Jayne,

Be unapol...
authentic, ...

Spiritual Nomad: A Journey Within and Abroad

Laura Vaisman

Some names and identifying details have been changed to protect the privacy of individuals.

SPIRITUAL NOMAD: A JOURNEY WITHIN AND ABROAD

Book Cover Design by Curtis Miller, CM Designs

Photos of Laura Vaisman: Jesus Baez, BAEZ Photography

Prologue

"The meaning of my life is to help others find the meaning of theirs"
-Viktor Frankl, 'A Man's Search for Meaning'

What was once a dead man's journey has now become my own. There was an old house with exposed brick and blue shutters with a big sign of 'Estate Sale' in the front lawn. I felt a pull to stop and check it out. I walked through the house as if I was searching for a hidden treasure. I walked upstairs. Each stair creaked, I found a small room in the attic with boxes filled with books and old film photography equipment. I stumbled upon a black journal. I dusted it off and turned each page and saw it was this man's travel journey through Italy and Switzerland. A deep surge of knowing my dreams would come true came over me. I was in the process of getting my Italian citizenship to eventually travel and move to Switzerland. The death of this man planted a seed into my soul to help me find the meaning of my life. On the next page after his last trip in Lugano, Switzerland I'd begin my own travel journey.

I was struggling with anxiety and yearned to see the world. I received a surprise opportunity for a solo trip to Europe, which crumbled the world I hid behind. I grew confident in letting my voice be heard and made a promise to myself to go to Europe again the following year alone and stay longer. I came back to the United States a new person, ready to conquer more of my fears and continue to see the world.

Unfortunately, life threw me a curve ball when I experienced a traumatic event with my brother that shook me to my core. Anxiety took over and I found it difficult to find the strength to go on and questioned everything. I struggled to leave the house and my fire for traveling was slowly burning out. As I began to emerge from a dark place and embarked on a journey within to love myself again, I learned to embrace my anxiety. I lusted to find love and feared no one could love a traveler. I welcomed the lessons life had to offer: the good, the bad, and the ugly.

In high school, I was a quiet girl. People knew who I was, but I chose to stay quiet. I would even play a game with myself to see how long I could go without speaking. Looking back on it, it was a way of meditation. There were some instances where teachers would mark me absent even though I was sitting in plain sight.

My mind was filled with racing thoughts and opinions, but I would never voice them because I cared too much about what other people thought. The only place where my voice was loud and heard was in my writing.

Everything changed when I took my first trip to Europe. It was a tour with an organization called People to People, where we spent twenty days traveling through six different countries. After the People to People trip, I broke out of my shell. I became more outspoken and confident. I was slowly becoming more like the real me.

In Europe, I was challenged with being outside of my comfort zone on a daily basis. I was in places where I didn't know the language or the culture, and I was surrounded by people I didn't know. I became fascinated with being unrecognizable.

Visiting each new place was a chance to start over; be reborn. It forced me to break out of my shy girl persona a little more, each time I traveled. I wanted to talk to people, find out who they were, and where they came from. I wanted to know everything about their culture. I was *hooked*.

I promised myself the next year, as a graduation gift to myself, I would backpack throughout Europe for two months alone. I was just graduating high school, confused and not sure what I wanted to do with my life. Enamored with the endless experiences and lessons I gained from traveling, I had an internal fire pushing me towards something. My father, of course, was not keen on the idea of his eighteen year old daughter backpacking alone around Europe. I understood his concern, but I was adamant about going. Ultimately, my cousin, Mike decided to come with me because he too, always wanted to do a Euro trip. We spent two months traveling through Europe by train, not having a clue about what we would get ourselves into.

This book is broken up into twelve chapters, each corresponding with a trip I've taken and the life lessons it taught me. The goal of this book is to show you anything your heart desires can indeed come true despite some bumps in the road. When your heart and soul are the driving force, you have to listen to them; let your inner compass guide you. With hard work, dedication, and a little bit of faith, I know your dreams can come true, too. My hope for you is to gain insight, confidence, and inspiration to do what you love. If you stop even for one second while reading this book, and think that maybe it can happen, then I've done my job. We are not bound to anything – the opportunities are limitless, and when you take the first leap, the universe, God or whatever force you believe in, will be there to catch you.

Life is way too short to hold back from living the life you want. I am deeply grateful for every travel experience I've embarked on. Each trip has challenged and molded me, giving me the greatest gift I could receive: growth. I still continue to travel today, and I will never stop. And hopefully, by the end of this book, you will feel inspired to venture on your own journey. I invite you to chase your dreams with me even in the face of your struggles. I want you to write everything down, write to me, tell me your travel experiences and how you've grown. It doesn't have to be far and wide. It can be to another state or the next country on your bucket list. Hell, maybe it's not even traveling but simply deciding to live your truth.

Chapter 1: Europe, or a Used Car?

2007

"A sense of humor is part of the art of leadership, of getting along with people, of getting things done."-President Eisenhower

At seventeen years old, I had a choice: A used car, or a trip to Europe. One of my high school teachers, I still don't know who, nominated me for the program, European Heritage. I remember sitting in this big auditorium listening to all the details of a twenty-day trip to six countries in Europe. While all of my friends were getting their licenses, permits and cars, I had one of my dreams sitting in the palm of my hand.

When I was little, I was always obsessed with Europe, especially London. I loved the people's accent and the way they enunciated certain words. Each word they spoke came out so beautifully. I remember being about ten years old and my sister had a work colleague visiting the States from London. My sister invited her to her house for us to meet her for dinner.

My eyes lit up in excitement to speak with her and ask her all about her country. I loved how different everything was compared to my life in the states. I couldn't have cared less about having a car – this was worth so much more. I told my dad I wanted this instead. He said it would be an early graduation gift, which I deeply appreciated then and still do today. It would be my first time going abroad alone.

Prior to leaving, several other kids and their parents from all over NJ came to meet in Monroe, NJ for monthly meetings. My dad and I would drive once a month together. We'd drive past beautiful parks and a cute main street in town to a community center. The building had white bricks and tall pole with the American flag flying in the wind. I was apprehensive as I walked inside.

I saw a group of kids I didn't know and parents mingling with the other parents over coffee and snacks. None of us knew each other but these would be the people I'd be traveling with. People to People prides themselves on making sure its students are educated about the places they visit, as well as guiding us to keep an open mind and help bring an understanding to the people we may meet. Each weekend we met and it was an all-day event to study each country we were going to.

We had group projects and we would have to find time to meet each other to get to know each other and also do the homework assignment. My group had Switzerland. Emma, Kelly, Annie, and myself were to find three facts about the country we found interesting and explain why. We barely knew anything about Switzerland except for it being famous for Swiss cheese. We all exchanged numbers and figured out whose house was the mid-way point, and we'd go to a local library to do our research.

We all met at a local library in a town called Franklin, NJ. A decent-sized town with lots of farm land nearby. I drove by rows of cornfields and some farmers market stands filled with fresh picked fruits and vegetables. All of us were the same age. We came up to the library one by one and awkwardly tried to get to know each other. I asked if anyone knew anything about Switzerland. We all looked at each other with inquisitive expressions on our faces and said no not really. We researched "cool things about Switzerland" and found out that Switzerland is a neutral country and doesn't get involved in wars, the Swiss put big cow bells on their cows so the farmers know where their cattle roam, and they speak five different languages.

The next weekend, it was our turn to present our country. Listening to other groups present their country, I was learning more and more about each place we were going to visit and the more the anticipation was rising. On top of projects, we volunteered as a group with our parents to local soup kitchens to help our own communities. The importance of educating ourselves about foreign countries and what was happening in our own backyard would later make sense that we are all one.

The day of the departure, my dad drove me to the airport where we met up with the rest of the group. It was a chaotic scene with forty or so people trying to figure out details of our flight and double and triple checking everyone was there before we left. We were given burgundy shirts to wear with "People to People" written in white lettering so we would recognize each other when we landed. Over the course of the last few months meeting in Monroe, we formed friendships and we didn't feel like strangers anymore. Because we all were closer, kids in my group, including myself, were even more excited. Before we were headed to security, everyone was hugging their parents and saying their "I love you's." My dad said he always wanted to take a trip like this, I felt a part of me was doing this for him, too. We said our goodbyes with a big hug and he told me to have a good time. From there, we all boarded the flight and we were on our way!

**

A group of Jersey kids, jetlagged and unfamiliar with what was to come, landed in Zurich, Switzerland. I noticed how beautiful the airport was. It was modern and so clean. As we formed as a group and went to find our checked luggage, the door opened and a breeze of air came through. It smelled so crisp and fresh. Coming from NJ, I wasn't used to smelling fresh air like that. We handed our luggage to our bus driver as quickly as we could and squeezed through the doors to claim our seat. I sat with my newfound best friend, Emma and I told her, "Let's sit in the front where Dominik is sitting." Dominik was our tour manager who was from Vienna, Austria. He spoke English well; he was tall with short messy hair yet somehow pulled it off to look sexy. He had a great smile and he was just… different. His accent was something I could describe as vaguely British and he wasn't like any of the guys back in the States or NJ. Like all the girls in our group, I had a crush on him but as usual I kept to myself and didn't make it known to anyone, except Emma who would later be my best keeper of secrets. I watched all the girls attempting to sit next to him on the bus, telling them stories about themselves to impress him, flirting to get his attention. It was like watching animals in heat. I just sat back and observed.

It wasn't like me to be forward when I found someone attractive. My heart would flutter every time he looked my way, but other girls would block my view. It started with catching each other's eye along with shy smiles. I was intrigued yet cautious because I didn't want to get in trouble from the director of our group for flirting with the tour manager and potentially get sent home. Angela was an art teacher who boasted her knowledge of the arts and painters. Her hair was always perfectly slicked back into a chignon; she wore her dress pants a little bit above her navel with a fanny pack hanging on her hip. Her makeup was flawlessly painted on her face every morning. She was a "by the books" kind of lady. We all were a little afraid of her to some degree, but what she didn't know couldn't hurt her.

While everyone else slept during long hauls from one city to the next, Dominik and I would talk for hours. He sat in front of me and I rested my arms on top of his headrest. We'd talk about life in Europe and America, how much I wanted to live in Europe and if he could just kidnap me and never let me go. As I laid my head on my arms to hear him speak of Europe and his life in Vienna, it was like being sung a lullaby, I was enamored by it all. His hand would gently brush across mine and I'd quickly move my hand away in fear that someone would see. My stomach rushed with butterflies. *Did he mean to do that?*

A little before heading into the capital of Bern, we stopped in Brienz, a small Swiss village right out of a storybook. The scenery was magical: Swiss chalets, tiny roads, and hundreds of window baskets overflowing with beautiful flowers. We stopped to watch a local Swiss shop owner hand carve a piece of wood into a bear, which is the symbol of Bern. Dominik and I would walk amongst the group trying not to make things obvious. I'd try my best to stand on opposite sides of the room so I could look at him from afar and not anger Angela. Dominik would be cheeky and try to find some way to get my attention by looking at me and smiling. I could see

Angela's face giving both of us the death stare.

We quickly gathered our things and ran back to the bus. I was excited to go back to my seat because I knew Dominik and I would have at least a few hours to talk. We were headed to Heidelberg, Germany to see their famous castle. I had never seen a real castle before and especially such an old one. Heidelberg is a small village with bridges over the river into town where there's cobblestone roads and tiny shops. The castle cannot be missed. A beautiful castle sitting up on a hilltop some parts demolished from the war with the French.

We got off the bus after a long four-hour drive from Switzerland. Emma and I hopped off to stretch our legs and we saw this long vertical walk to the top of the stairs to enter the castle. There was even a metal railing on the side if you were struggling to walk up the hill. I tried my best to push through it because a small part of me didn't want Dominik to think I was a stereotypical lazy American. I heard that quite a bit when I was in Europe. Oh, and that we're loud, which I agree with. Anyway, I proved my point and the hike was worth it. The view from the hilltop was spectacular. I saw a majority of Heidelberg and the riverboat tours float by.

We were scheduled for a tour of the castle where we learned about the history; some of the rooms had the original beds where the king slept. As the tour was going on, I could sense Dominik walking towards me. I felt closer to him after having many talks on the bus for hours and felt a little bit more comfortable flirting back, even with Angela there. I said, "Can we live here together in this big castle?" He laughed, smiled back, and said, "Of course, I will buy you this castle so you could be my princess." My heart melted.

It had only been a couple days in from first arriving in Europe and I didn't want it to end. I was learning so much in such a short period of time. We visited a German farmer who gathered his own milk straight from his cows while his wife prepared homemade apple cinnamon bread with fresh ingredients from her garden. I couldn't refuse a glass of fresh milk straight from the cow. Being lactose intolerant, I was scared of the consequences but was surprised that I was able to handle it. The bread was phenomenal; it had swirls of cinnamon and bits of apple. I was amazed by the generosity of strangers who went out of their way to make us foreigners feel welcome in their country. I was in love with the unknown. Traveling broke the barrier for me, transformed the high school girl who rarely spoke up, rarely questioned anything to being curious and vocal.

***

Still in Germany, we went to a youth hostel in the Black Forest region. The trees were a dark green color and being so closely bunched together they resembled almost a black color. You could see it for miles. The youth hostel was cool for us because they had games and lots of activities to do outside. I was roomed in this big dorm-style room with six bunk beds. We weren't allowed to choose who we roomed with so people wouldn't continue to room with the same people, and/or, could cause trouble. A bunch of us girls hung out inside the room for a bit and everyone was gossiping on how cute Dominik was. I was unpacking my stuff and overheard the conversation, but I didn't want anyone to know of the connection he and I had. Some girls were suspicious and would ask if I liked him, but I'd say no.

We sat near the window after unpacking and looked into the field where Dominik was playing football (soccer, for Americans) with some of the boys. The girls said, "Let's go play and have a girls vs. boys game." We ran downstairs and challenged them to a game. I never played sports in school, but I loved being athletic. Our first game was fun. Some girls didn't know how to play but Dominik asked me if I had played before. I said, "No." He said, "You seem like you have some natural ability then. Maybe one day you'll play for the Women's German team." I laughed, smiled for a few moments to distract him, and then stole the ball right under his feet, scoring the goal for the girls. The girls ran up to me and we all cheered. Eventually we won. The boys wanted to have a coed game next round. We all lined up waiting to be picked. The girls were whispering, "Oh, I hope Dominik picks me to be on his team."

In my mind, I wondered if he'd pick me, but I didn't voice it to anyone. It was down to me, a couple girls and boys. The girls were looking at me to see if I would show any signs of my fondness towards Dominik. Then Dominik called out, "Vaisman! Get on my team." I could feel the girl's eyes glaring at me.

We were playing on grass. I took my shoes off because I couldn't play as well in flip flops. Dominik said, "Won't that hurt your feet to kick the ball?" I said, "No I'll be fine. I'm helping you out because now we'll win."

There was one girl who wasn't keen on Dominik's attention towards me. The game started, I had the ball, and Dominik and a few other boys ran to the other end goal. The girl was gunning for me and stole the ball. I ran as fast as I could to her and stole the ball back. I shot it all the way to Dominik and he scored a goal. We started a new play and this time Dominik and the boys led while I tried to make my way to cover our goal. The girl had the ball and I ran up to her to try to get it from her. Our feet were moving almost like dancing. The girl kicked the ball as hard as she could into my shins where it almost took me down and then she hit me again with it while I was trying to get my balance. I could tell this was more than competitiveness. The football game went on and the other team wound up winning by one.

It was getting close to dinner time so we stopped. As we walked back, Dominik could tell I was down about the defeat. He put his arm over my shoulder and said, "Don't worry about it. It's just a game."

I said, "I know, I get competitive sometimes. I'll be fine."

As much as I wanted Dominik's affection, I wished he was more discreet so no one else would notice. The girls in the group only grew more suspicious and rumors started to spread.

When we got back to our rooms to freshen up some of us stayed in the common area of our room to chat. Our door opened slightly and it was our bus driver. He wasn't very friendly to begin with, so I found it strange he was there. The bus driver asked how our day was and how we were liking Germany so far. The girls entertained the conversation. I sat back and observed. Then out of nowhere he said, "It'd be better if you all were naked."

The girls were speechless but I immediately said, "Hey! You need to get the fuck out!" He was startled by my reaction and quickly left. We shut the door and locked it. I said, "Stay in here and I'm going to tell someone." I ran to Dominik in the hall and told him what had happened. He was shocked and said he will handle it.

We all headed down to the dining hall to have dinner. They shut the doors for privacy and I could tell Angela and the chaperones were flustered. They told us due to the recent incident with the bus driver, he would no longer be driving us. Everyone knew prior to sitting down. News traveled fast. We all applauded and cheered. A boy in the group asked where he was going to stay? Angela said he would not be staying at this hostel and would take a bus in town back home. And she assured us not to worry and to report anything that is inappropriate. We'd have our new driver in the morning.

***

Our next stop was lovely Paris. My only knowledge of what Paris could be like was from movies and books. On our Parisian tour, we were going to check off seeing the palace of Versailles, the Louvre, Mona Lisa and, of course, The Eiffel tower.

Unfortunately, it was pouring cats and dogs when we arrived at Versailles. We were signed up to do a group tour throughout the palace. We all wore headphones and were able to walk freely listening to the tour guide tell us the history. We tried to stay together in a group, but to say it was absolutely packed was an understatement. Our tour guide was this tiny

French woman and I lost the group and her in the crowd. I stumbled upon the hall of mirrors. It reminded me of the ballroom in the movie *Beauty and the Beast*. It was filled with mirrors on every piece of wall, gigantic crystal chandeliers hanged from the ceilings, and were filled with gold antiquities. I got lost in its beauty and then I heard static in my headphones and a woman saying, *"This way"* with a French accent.

I tried to follow what she was saying to gather any clue as to where the group was. I caught her saying *"Mona Lisa."* I asked someone for a map to find the room where the Mona Lisa was. I ran there as quickly as I could in order to not lose them again. I saw some of my friends and Dominik saw me running all flustered. He smiled at me and shook his head. He said, "Where were you?"

I said, "I lost the group in the crowd and then got distracted by the hall of mirrors." He smiled and said, "Stay close to the group this time."

The Mona Lisa was quite anti-climactic because I was standing behind a massive crowd of people and couldn't see where it was. I expected it to be a huge painting, but it was small. We continued our tour through The Louvre fighting through crowds of people and learning French history.

After, we grabbed a small bite to eat at the café nearby before we headed towards the Eiffel Tower. Granted, we were traveling at the height of the season, but the lines to all the tourist areas were unbelievable. Sometimes, it was better to travel with a company or a big group because we got perks of cutting the line. When we got off the bus, I could see *the* Eiffel tower ahead.

Again, a lot smaller than I expected, but without a doubt, it's a beautiful site to see. Emma, myself, a few other girls, and Dominik squeezed into an elevator that brought us to the top. We didn't want to go to the third level because it was too windy. We were on the second level and I could feel the tower swaying a tiny bit. The girls and I were taking silly group photos with Paris in the background. Out the corner of my eye, I could see Dominik walking around. We locked eyes and I could see the girls were having fun and distracted so I walked off on my own towards where he was. He smiled and said, "Hi."

I smiled and told him how beautiful Paris was. We walked around to the other side of the tower because Angela and the other counselors were above on the third level watching the group. In the field below, I pointed out a heart that was carved into the grass. I said, "How cute is that!"

We stared out into the city looking through big binoculars. I was looking around at all the couples holding hands walk by. I laughed and said, "Don't you think it's kinda cliché and stupid to propose on the Eiffel Tower?"

Dominik said, "Would you think it's stupid if I asked you?"

My stomach filled with butterflies and my eyes widened in surprise as to what I had just heard. I nervously laughed not knowing what to say and smiled, "I guess not."

We didn't have much time to spend in Paris so unfortunately; it was time to get back on the bus and head to Belgium. A four-hour ride was nice compared to the long stretches we had done lately. We were sleepy from a long day of running around Paris. How many times can you say, *"Oh please forgive me, I was absolutely exhausted from running around Paris all day."* No one was complaining.

Angela set in place a number system where we would do a count off to make sure everyone was on the bus or in the group wherever we were. Angela would scream, *"One!"* to get the person assigned to number one to start off. Our unassigned seats became permanent seats for the rest of the trip. The group was starting to split amongst older and younger kids in the group. Some of us were seventeen and eighteen and others were sixteen and younger. Tension started to grow solely from a maturity level. The kids in the back were the young ones, when someone wasn't paying attention and messed up the numbers. Angela would yell, "*Nope! Let's try that again!*" Didn't matter what number we were at. Us older kids would get frustrated because the bus couldn't leave until we all were accounted for. "*One!*", Angela yelled again. The number sequence would begin. I was number thirty-seven and I was hoping to not have any mess ups. We got to forty without a single mess up and Angela yelled, "*Yeah Ho!*", which signaled Dominik to tell the bus driver to get going.

I tried to stay up as long as I could because Dominik and I wanted to chat. I had a gray fuzzy neck pillow that was so comfortable you'd instantly go to sleep. I'd keep it around my neck sometimes for warmth and I was distracted talking to Emma who always sat next to me on the bus. We were giggling and gossiping around the other girls in the group when someone snatched my neck pillow off of my neck. I gasped and looked around and I noticed Dominik had it. I leaped over the seat. He held it for dear life and said, "But it's so comfortable!"

I laughed and went to reach for it again but he grabbed my hand and wouldn't let it go. I was in an awkward position of half my body leaning over his seat and him holding my hand. I began to blush and my heart raced. His smile made him even more kissable. He pulled me closer and we almost bumped heads. I got a whiff of his cologne and commented on how good it smelled. He said it was CK One. I smiled back at him and snatched my pillow. I fell back into my seat and put the pillow around my neck. All I could smell was his cologne.

***

We stayed one night in the outskirts of Paris. This time we got the surprise on the bus that we could pick our roommates. Emma and I immediately hugged each other until we got the okay to go and find our room. We got settled and were so relieved to room together and not have to deal with the drama from the other girls in the group. I told her I was going for a walk to write in my travel journal for a little bit. Twenty days with forty plus people was a bit overwhelming.

It was night time and I walked out of the hotel into the front and found a garden with some benches. Unbeknownst to me, Dominik was outside as well. It was beginning to hit me that I'd be leaving to go home and back to school to start my senior year of high school. All I wanted to do was stay in Europe and travel. After writing pages and pages of my time on this trip and all the amazing things I've experienced, I headed back to my room to freshen up. Emma asked where I was. I said, "In the garden. Why?" Emma sighed and told me not to get upset. I braced myself for what she was about to tell me.

She said, "You may be in trouble. A girl saw you walk outside and then shortly after Dominik did the same. So now Angela thinks you two ran off somewhere."

Tears welled up in my eyes. Emma consoled me. I told her I wasn't with him, I was writing in my journal and I didn't even know he was outside. Emma said, "I know, I believe you."

I said to her, "Even if there was something I was doing I'd at the very least tell you because I know you'd cover for me." I was frustrated and emotional. I went to take a shower to cool off and relax before going to bed.

A few moments into my shower, Emma poked her head in the door and said, "Angela is at the door. She wants to know that you're here." I said, "Well I'm in the shower." And yelled out, "It's me. I'm just taking a shower."

I could hear Angela firmly tell Emma, "I need proof."

I then got out of the shower and stuck my fingers through the door for her to see and said, "It's me, Laura. I'm taking a shower."

Angela said, "Poke your head through the door."

I did as she asked but I was furious. Emma and I spoke after Angela left. I said, "Really? What is her problem?"

Emma said, "I know that was a little ridiculous. I told her you were here. She didn't believe me."

In this particular People to People program, you received a pass/fail in order to receive college credit. I told Emma I wouldn't jeopardize not passing to do something stupid like that. Emma tried to make light of the situation and said, "I mean it is really cute how fond Dominik is of you." I awkwardly smiled to appease her attempt to change the subject and went to bed after having an emotional night.

***

We got word that we were heading to Belgium. I didn't know much about Belgium except for Belgian waffles and chocolate. When we arrived in Bruges, we stopped at a local doily shop to learn about the history of doilies and how they were made. I had a difficult time paying attention because I could smell fresh Belgian waffles being made around the corner. I whispered to Dominik if me and Emma could run to get one. He said, "You can, just be quick and come right back."

Me and Emma slowly moved closer to the door trying not to make it obvious and when everyone was focused on doilies, we bolted. Our noses followed the sweet trail of sugar to a small shop. The line was almost out the door, the back was lined with multiple waffle makers sizzling with ooey goodness. The waffles were warm and each bite was light, airy, and delicious. It didn't need anything else put on it but we asked for Nutella, which seeped into the little pockets of the waffle… its warm chocolatey-hazelnutty flavor only made it more heavenly. Emma and I were busy basking in the deliciousness of eating our waffles that we lost track of time. We turned around and Dominik was standing there with his hands on his hips, shaking his head. Emma and I smiled at him, laughed, and said, "Sorry! But did you try the waffle? It's amazing." Dominik smirked. I then told him, "Here, take a bite of mine." Dominik obliged and his eyes rolled back into his head as he exclaimed, "WOW!" Emma and I laughed.

I said, "See! I told you it was worth us missing out on seeing how Doilies were made." Dominik chuckled and told us to get going because we had a horse and carriage ride around the city. The group split into two. Emma and I ran to the first carriage to be with our other friends. The horse was beautiful with a white coat, the hair on his hooves were grown out a bit longer with brown coating. It almost resembled the horse wearing shoes.

There were plenty of pinchable moments where I thought I was stuck in a dream. Bruges looks like a medieval fairytale. From the cobblestone roads, buildings that go as far back as to the 13th century and romantic canals. Dominik was quite the photographer amongst the group. He had a fancy camera that he'd take with him everywhere. He was on the second carriage behind us and when they caught up alongside of us, he'd try to get a picture of me. I'd make a silly face or cover my face, but there were times where he took beautiful candid shots of me throughout the trip and share with me later on the bus. Our time in Belgium was short. We had to get back on the bus again and head to The Netherlands.

Amsterdam was more than just weed. You could smell it in the air from time to time but I wasn't intrigued by it. We weren't allowed free time in Amsterdam for obvious reasons. We had plans to visit the Anne Frank house and a cheese factory. First, cheese. And sadly, I wasn't able to have it but for you cheese lovers, who doesn't love cheese? We walked into a small blue factory that looked like a house on the outside. It was run by a husband and wife who made cheese from scratch. Some from herbs picked from their garden. We were able to pick three cheeses we wanted to take home a gift for visiting. I picked two plain regular ones and stinging nettle as the other. Back when we were in Germany, we came across stinging nettle the hard way after walking through a field of it. Hence the name, 'stinging,' you would notice a strong stinging sensation for a few minutes, but it's definitely not pleasant. Some kids in the group thought it would be funny to have a stinging nettle fight. Not fun.

Anyway, the wife ensured us that we would not experience the same sensation eating the cheese. The husband showed us his woodshop where he would handmake wooden clogs. I picked one to take home with me. It was painted red with flowers and infamous windmills and mine happened to be a piggy bank.

The husband asked us if we had any questions. I asked, "What makes you happy?"

The husband pondered for a moment and said, "This."

I said, "Clogs?"

The husband shook his head and smiled. And said, "It is sharing my passion with you all or anyone who comes into my shop. My wife and I built this clog and cheese factory from the ground up. To see the curious looks on your faces and how excited you all get to watch me build you clogs or for my wife to make you cheese warms my heart.

When you're passionate about something, your happiness radiates to others, so make sure to share it."

We applauded and thanked them for giving us a tour. We slowly took our gifts and souvenirs and headed towards the exit. Outside, there were two gigantic yellow clogs, big enough that you could put your entire foot in with lots of room to spare. I saw Dominik behind me and signaled him to come outside. I laughed and said, "You have to get in the shoes and let me take a picture of you."

He was reluctant and said, "I look horrible in pictures."

I smirked, "You've been taking pictures of me this entire trip, the least you could do is let me take *one* picture of you."

He smiled, bowed his head in defeat, and slowly climbed into the shoes. The shoes on him looked like he had big Mickey Mouse feet but they just happened to be yellow clogs. I laughed because he looked so cute yet so annoyed at the same time.

We still had a lot of daytime left and we were told we had a bicycle tour along the river and windmills. The

Netherlands was also known for millions of bikes. Almost everyone has one and they even have parking garages for bicycles and they are filled to the brim. There were a couple kids in our group that didn't know how to ride a bike. We busted their chops and told them, "You gotta learn now." They laughed nervously as they attempted to get on a bike for the first time. Emma, myself and couple of other girls got a head start.

We biked a narrow asphalt trail surrounded by canals on both sides. There were wooden windmills turning in the wind in the distance. The breeze blew through my hair and the sun warmed my cheeks. Emma came racing by and interrupted my daydreaming trance and yelled, "Come on slowpoke!"

I pedaled faster to catch up to her and looked behind me and no one was there. I yelled out to Emma, "Hey! We have to stop, we're going too far ahead." We stopped and waited a quite a while. We wondered what was taking everyone so long.

In the distance, I could see Dominik riding up the pathway towards us. I thought, *Anything he does is sexy.* I shook myself out of daydreaming and asked what happened.

Dominik said, "Someone fell into the river."

I burst out laughing and questioned how that happened. He said it was one of kids who didn't know how to ride a bike. She couldn't figure out how to use her brakes, panicked, and drove straight into the river.

Still laughing, he signaled us to drive back to her to help her out. By the time we arrived, we saw a girl pushing her bike up the hill dripping wet. We helped her out and asked a nearby shop if they had any towels. The girl was upset and embarrassed. We tried laughing and joking with her to ease her embarrassment. I said, "Well, now you'll never forget riding a bike for the first time in The Netherlands. Not many people can say they fell into a river canal in The Netherlands."

She smiled and we all hugged her and said not to worry about it. The other chaperones stayed with her as she walked her bike back to the beginning of the trail. We had to hurry back on to the bus because we had to make our overnight ferry to London. England would be our last stop before heading back to NJ. Emma and a group of girls I consistently hung out with during the trip, were huddled outside the bus taking pictures. I suggested we go by the water because it was a prettier background than the bus. Then it was a full-on photoshoot. We took a bunch of silly group pictures and then walked to the ferry. Since it was already quite late, we all went to bed.

I've always wanted to go to England since I was little. I wanted to have tea time and do as the Brits do. We had to wake up early in the morning once our ferry arrived in London. The chaperones told us to wear our dressy clothes for today because we will be going to a play later. I also had a deep love for Shakespeare and we were told we'd be seeing Romeo and Juliet but it's different and that part they were keeping a surprise. But first, we went to Buckingham Palace where the queen and the royal family reside. It's a beautiful building protected by armed royal guards. The chaperones told us, "I know you guys will want to mess with the guards but do not do it." They do not move a muscle or show any emotion. It was tempting to try to make one of the guards crack, but we took pictures instead.

We walked as a group to Hyde Park to take pictures on the bridge. Emma and the group of girls we hung out with had another photoshoot in our fancy clothes. I then asked Angela if we were going to have English tea time. She said no. My jaw dropped and I said, "What? How can we come to England and not have tea and scones?" She said, "We don't have enough time, we have to go to the London Eye and then make our play." My inner dream of having a full out English experience was crushed.

We boarded the bus to drive to the London Eye. As you approach there is no missing it. It's huge with giant clear capsules filled with people to overlook the city. Angela screamed, "ONE!"

And the count off began. It was a little embarrassing to do in public. A group of Americans screaming out numbers. She said we will all most likely be separated on the London eye so partner up and stick together and we'll regroup after the ride is over. I purposely didn't go into the capsule where Dominik was. I was beginning to get a bit weary and I could feel Angela watching me like a hawk.

The London eye is a giant ferris wheel that moves extremely slow so no matter which capsule you're in you'll get the same view. Emma and I ran to the end of the capsule to check out the view. Our capsules made it to the top and the view was beautiful, I could see the infamous clock tower, Big Ben. Some moments the ride would stop to let people on and off. We could see part of our group in other capsules and we'd make funny faces at each other. Slowly, our capsule made it back down to the ground and we had to wait for the others to get off. I was chatting with Emma and was ecstatically telling her how I can't wait for the Shakespeare play. She laughed and said it should be fun.

As the remainder of the group got off the London Eye, we had to do the embarrassing count-off again. Once everyone was accounted for, we went back on the bus to drive to the play. As we drove, I was just a kid in a candy store and pointed out every little thing that was different or British. I'd say, "Oh my God, we're driving on the other side of the road," or "There are the cute red phone booths!" Everyone in my front section of the bus would laugh at my childlike excitement.

When we arrived, I saw the sign that said Shakespeare play comedy. I was confused and thought how could they make a comedy out of *Romeo and Juliet*? As we each hopped off the bus, I noticed the red phone booth out of the corner of my eye and cued Emma and the girls to take pictures. The door was heavy to open and unfortunately the booth smelled like piss. I signaled to Emma to hurry up and take the picture because I was holding my breath. Angela yelled for us to come back to the group. We all stood around and Dominik said he had our tickets. Angela said, "So line up and he'll hand them out." In my mind I wanted to sit next to him but I knew that wouldn't be a good idea since the tension about him and I was at an all-time high at this point in our trip. We anxiously waited and took our tickets and went into the theatre. There were balcony seats and some others below. Dominik gave me my ticket last as we walked in and my heart sank to my stomach in a mix of happiness and fear. Dominik gave me the ticket to sit right next to him. Angela sat across from us on the opposite side of the balcony and we both felt her angry glare. I whispered, "Dominik! Now you've made it absolutely obvious. Angela is furious."

Dominik said, "Who cares! I wanted to sit next to you and enjoy these last few moments with you. And she can't blame you this time because I passed out the tickets." He put his hand on my leg in reassurance, smiled, and said, "Let's just enjoy the show."

The show consisted of bad makeup, wigs, and inappropriate jokes but it was brilliant. The show poked fun at the story of *Romeo and Juliet*. In the last scene, Romeo finds

Juliet dead and as he is about to take his own life, he stops and says, *"You know what Juliet? This is rubbish. I know you're alive… cut the shit."* It was a hilarious spin of one of Shakespeare's classic romances. We all laughed until tears streamed down our faces. Out of the corner of my eye, I could see Dominik laughing as well but looking at me as he put his arm around me. Overwhelmed with joy and sadness, I started thinking I didn't want this to end. I was beginning to understand that my intuition tells me when I'm in the right place; it's an unbelievable amount of peace and the purest of joy where nothing in the world can disturb your peace.

***

When the play was over, we left the theatre to have our final dinner in London together. Everyone had grown so close together despite meeting as strangers. Traveling brings people of all kinds together and when you listen closely to their words, you find out how much you have in common. We all sat in this long wooden table eating our fish and chips, laughing, and swapping stories. I sat back and looked at everyone as if someone had pushed slow-mo, taking it all in, because I knew we were going home after dinner. It was like playing games outside when you were a little kid with your friends, having such a blast, and your mom calls you in for dinner. Angela and the other chaperones made a toast to everyone for a wonderful trip and thanking Dominik for planning the trip and being a great tour guide.

Our bags were already packed on the bus from the previous night and we were back on the bus, Angela did one last final count off before heading to the airport. Dominik came with us to say bye and see us off at the airport; we were flying back to NJ and Dominik was heading back home to Vienna, Austria. We arrived at one of London's main airports, Heathrow, and before heading to the security check in, the group charged towards Dominik to give him a big hug. I saw him look at me over their shoulders as I tried to hold back tears. Dominik came to me and we gave each other the biggest embrace. I told him, "I don't want to leave. Put me in your suitcase back to Austria."

He smiled and said, "I wish I could, but I think they'd flag my suitcase with you in it." We took our last photo together and exchanged emails to keep in touch. I told him, "I'm coming back next year when I graduate high school, mark my words."

He hugged me one more time and said, "You're my princess, remember that. I'll see you next summer."

Chapter 2: Nothing Lasts Forever

2008

"I can't think of anything that excites a greater sense of childlike wonder than to be in a country where you are ignorant of almost everything." Bill Bryson

My word to visit Europe again came true. I was about to graduate high school busting my ass working two jobs to save enough money to go backpacking through Europe. I wanted to go alone, but my parents weren't too keen on their eighteen year old daughter going to Europe by herself. I understood their concern but I was doing it, regardless of whether I had someone with me or not. Thankfully, Mike volunteered to come along since he always wanted to go backpacking.

When I landed back home in NJ from my first trip, I was disappointed I didn't see a message from Dominik in my inbox. I wasn't sure about emailing him. *Maybe he didn't want to talk to me. Will he think I'm annoying if I email him? Maybe he misspelled my email address.* Eventually, I built up the courage to email him back:

Subject: PRINCESS LAURA!!!

"Why didn't my email go through?! Ok, I'll try again. I clearly remember writing to you because I even missed my train from Vienna to Linz because I chose to finish your email instead. So, this is how much I miss you. How could you possibly think I wouldn't want to talk to you anymore! I still think I should have taken you with me in my hand luggage. So long my little princess. Love, Dominik"

I think you could have scooped me off the floor. I was elated to tell him I was coming to Europe and I'd visit him in Vienna. This was my first time going abroad with no curfews or rules like my People to People trip. I had no idea how to plan a trip like this, which made me anxious.

Prior to leaving for our trip, Mike and I met with my dad's friend who was an avid traveler. We visited his house after Mike and I spent hours in Barnes & Noble reading travel guide books researching where to go and what to see. We bought Rick Steve's travel maps, and my dad's friend recommended "must see" places to visit. I remember sitting at his dinner table when a rush of tightness came in my chest, my vision blurred, my heart raced, and my body tensed up. I didn't understand what was happening to me. Later in life, I would understand I was having an anxiety attack. I was overwhelmed by what we were doing, even though this was something I wanted badly.

Despite feeling anxious and scared, I made a promise to myself that I'd go back to Europe and more so I promised Dominik I'd come back. I pushed through the fear because I remembered how I felt when I traveled the year before. I had to remind myself that everything was going to work out the way it was supposed to. We had our maps all set; traced with an itinerary of places we wanted to visit. We purposefully made our plans flexible for any wild adventures.

We went to the mecca of camping stores in NJ called Campmor; it has everything and more: guidebooks, camping gear, sleeping bags, travel clothes, and so on. Mike and I needed backpacks, so we went there to get fitted for them to make sure they were comfortable enough to carry for our two-month trip. They put sandbags in to give the pack some weight to see how it felt. Mine was red, 65L Lowe Alpine pack. It had lots of pockets and my favorite part was the hip buckles so the weight wasn't all on your shoulders. We fell in love with our backpacks and bought them. Two hundred dollars later, everything was beginning to feel more real. I couldn't believe I was going backpacking in Europe for two months.

My family will take any reason to celebrate. They threw us a pleasant journey barbeque with close family and friends. Everyone wrote little notes of love and advice for us to carry with us on our trip. Some notes from my family stuck out and inspired me to stay on this path.

"My dear sister! Live! Like it's the last day! Love, like it's the only love! Stay curious, always question to gain more of your experiences and dive into the unknown, and be happy wherever you land!"

"No matter what you do in your career path or in life. BE PASSIONATE and have vigor in all you pursue. Be happy! And live life to its fullest. Love, Dad."

"Live with heart! Be grateful. Thank God. You are special. Love yourself. Believe in yourself. Follow your heart. Be kind. Listen. Dream and see it first then it will follow. I'm proud of you. Love, Mom"

We all ate delicious food cooked from my Argentinian father and Italian mother, from Argentinian style steaks smothered chimichurri sauce to homemade cacciatore. So, you can imagine the bliss we all were in. Everyone wished us luck and it was onto our journey to Frankfurt, Germany.

We arrived in Frankfurt and I wasn't feeling well, partially from anxiety, jet lag, and being in a foreign land. I didn't have an appetite at first, but we stopped in an adorable café to kill time because our check in wasn't until 2:00 p.m.. Being in Europe again without a rigid itinerary was refreshing. We had delicious margarita pizza and a big glass of German beer. Mike and I cheered our glasses together to celebrate the start of our two-month adventure.

We realized it was almost time to check into our hostel and we took a train to Frankfurt's main train station where we read from the hostel's website that the hostel was within walking distance from the station. We did not have cell phones and relied on our own research and or asking locals. We eventually found it and were surprised by the countless porn shops as we walked down the street and we found ourselves uneasy about staying in this area. Later, we found out it was in the middle of the red-light district, which is an area that contains sex shops, sex businesses and/or brothels. Luckily, we wouldn't be staying in Frankfurt long. We walked the streets passing sex shop after sex shop, carrying our heavy backpacks, not sure when we would find the hostel. I saw a small sign on the building for "Frankfurt Hostel" ahead and screamed in excitement, "I found it!"

Mike said, "Thank god!" We opened a big heavy Victorian door and walked down a beautiful corridor with marble floors and a spiral staircase. We looked around for an elevator but there wasn't one. Sweating and tired from our long travel day, we both sighed, "I guess we have to take the stairs."

Mike said, "Which floor is it?" I looked around and saw a sign that said, 'Frankfurt Hostel Floor 3.' I tilted my head back with despair and laughed, "Third floor." We slowly walked up three flights of stairs, laughing at how exhausted we were. We finally made it to the top and we felt like we had climbed Mt. Everest.

We were greeted by two friendly Germans and one of them asked, "Are you Laura?"

I said, "Yes, I have a reservation for two people."

They said, "We only have a dorm-style room." Mike and I couldn't care less, we just wanted a bed and a shower. The German guy introduced himself as Jonas and said, "That'll be twenty Euros." Jonas also informed us that today the hostel was hosting a spaghetti party.

I asked, "What is that?"

Jonas said, "We just make a shit ton of pasta for the guests."

Mike and I laughed. I said, "We'll be there."

Jonas gave us our keys and we walked down a mysteriously dark hallway and couldn't figure out why the lights wouldn't go on. As we continued down, they all flickered on. We were staying in a green (eco) hostel where they conserved energy on electricity and water. We opened the door to a ten-bed dorm. The dusty, old, moldy smell greeted our noses and our dorm mates introduced themselves and we all exchanged, 'Where are you from?' questions. They said they were both from Canada. The beds were shitty metal Ikea furniture with prison-like mattresses. I sat on the bed and the whole bunk moved and squeaked.

The other dorm mates said, "Yeah, it's fucking noisy in here." I couldn't complain too much, as twenty Euros for a hostel is cheap. Our dorm mates asked if we had any plans for tonight. Mike and I said no but we were going to hit up the spaghetti party and then go explore. The Canadians said, "We'll join you and do you both fancy watching the football game and grab some beers after?"

Mike and I looked at each and said, "Absolutely."

We locked our dorm room and walked to the common area where the spaghetti party was going down. As we walked down the hallway, the aroma of fresh pasta being made engulfed the room, and our mouths watered. We walked in and there were two gigantic pots of boiling pasta and huge bowls of spaghetti already made with an array of sauces to choose from. We filled our tummies with loads of pasta and then headed to the park nearby where the Canadians said the game was playing on a huge screen. The sun had gone down by the time we walked outside; there was a slight brisk in the air but it was nothing to complain about. People were lying in the grass with blankets holding their gigantic beer glasses cheering for their team. Mike and I grabbed the beers and the Canadians went to look for a place to sit. We sat, drank, laughed and cheered for Germany, of course.

In our tipsy state, we swayed our way home, laughing and cheering to other people about the game. When we got back to our hostel, we jumped into our noisy beds and attempted to sleep. I woke up exhausted and in pain from sleeping on what felt like a rock. Mike and I had a long travel day ahead as the next stop on our itinerary was The Mosel Valley. We hugged our Canadian dorm mates and I said, "Hopefully we'll bump into each other again."

We walked down to the Frankfurt main train station that was only a few minutes walk from our hostel. It was huge with beautiful metal beams and glass ceilings with an open vestibule for the trains to roll in. I felt like I was in another time period for a second. Mike and I traveled with nothing but our maps and guidebooks, and we had no clue where our train was. Not speaking a single word of German, I sat on the bench utterly confused, and Mike, a few feet from me, looked like a deer in headlights. I told Mike, "We should attempt to ask someone.

A train conductor has to speak at least a little bit of English." I looked through our guidebook for common phrases to use. I pointed it out to Mike and said ask this next train conductor this, "Sprechen du Englisch?" I giggled at our attempts to say it. I'm sure we butchered it but the conductor understood and said, "Yes, I speak a little English." Mike explained that we were trying to go to the Mosel Valley and he said to go to Track 3 and hurry because it was leaving soon. We grabbed our packs and ran towards Track 3, but we had no idea which direction to go.

We reached this big, long red train and Mike was on the ledge as I was running up to catch up to him. I looked at the sign and yelled to Mike, "Get off the train, that's going to PARIS!" He jumped off as the train was slowly moving. I said, "Now what?" We looked at our map and I said, "We could go to Heidelberg, I've been there before and it's an adorable little town and we can reconvene and figure out where we're going to next. Plus, we've been here the entire day."

Mike agreed and said, "Screw it, let's just go and we can find a place to stay there." We took a train to Heidelberg and all I could remember is the memories I had when I went last year with People to People and Dominik.

Exhausted from our long night of drinking, not sleeping on comfortable beds, and a long travel day, we stayed in a more expensive hotel. When we got to our room, we dropped our bags and plopped onto the bed. Lying on the beds felt like sleeping on plush clouds. We fell into a deep slumber before heading out to go explore. Summer was kicking into high gear and Germany was being hit with an unusual heatwave. My cousin couldn't take the heat anymore. Mike took out his shavers and started shaving his head. I laughed in surprise as he started to shave his head into a mohawk. Mike said, "What? I'll be less hot."

I shook my head saying, "Whatever floats your boat."

***

As we walked to Schloss Heidelberg, I was reminded of my conversation with Dominik. *"Can we live here together in this big castle?"* He *laughed, smiled back, and said, "Of course, I will buy you this castle so you could be my princess."* Mike and I booked a tour to learn about the castle's history and we had a hilarious guide who had a slight aversion to the French. In the 17th century the castle was repeatedly attacked by the French during The War of the Grand Alliance, which unfortunately destroyed parts of the castle. We had a few French tourists in our group and the guide said, "We would have this beautiful part of the castle to show you but now it's only parts of it because the French destroyed it." Everyone tried not to look at the French tourists but we all did it at some point. Their faces were appalled at the guide's playful remarks, which only made some of us giggle.

After the tour, we were free to roam the castle premises as long as we wanted. Mike and I hung around for a bit and a bunch of Japanese tourists with big cameras around their necks ran up to Mike as if he were a celebrity. We were both caught off guard. We smiled to be polite and gestured if they wanted us to take a picture for them. They didn't speak any English but laughed, pointed at Mike's hair, and lifted their camera. They wanted to take a picture because of his mohawk. I stood to the side to let Mike have his paparazzi shot as I laughed behind the group of people.

We left as fast as we could before we got stopped by more tourists. We found a trail called, 'Philosophical Walk' and slowly we ascended to the top of the mountain on the opposite side of the river. The sun was beginning to set. Pinks and oranges glowed over the Castle Heidelberg. We sat at a bench to catch our breath and take in the beauty. A man walked up to us and asked if we were a couple. Mike and I laughed, "No we're cousins." He was embarrassed and offered to take our picture with the castle in the background. He introduced himself and said he was a photographer and would take a nice photo for us. He asked for my email and said he'd send it after he edits it. He wished us luck on our journey.

I said, "So you know we can't stay at this hotel. It's ninety euros a night and we're on a tight budget."

Mike sighed, "I know, but those beds are so comfortable. But I agree, we need to find another hostel in Heidelberg."

We happened to find a new place to stay near the largest zoo in Europe. The hostel was a lot cheaper with animals making noises all night long. I was woken up the next morning by what sounded like a dying cat. I opened the window blinds to find a huge peacock sitting on the windowsill! Terrified and confused, I went to the common area to find Mike having a beer with a guy he met watching the football match. "Starting early, huh?"

Mike said, "Yeah, fuck it, come and have a morning beer," as he chuckled mid-sentence and waved for me to come over. Mike introduced me to his new-found friend, Ludwig. He said hi and offered to buy me a beer. Ludwig asked what I liked. I said, "I don't know." I tried whatever Mike had and it was delicious. Mike said Ludwig had offered to drive us to Munich since he was heading that way anyway and would drop us off in the main part of the city. I tilted my head a little bit and gave Mike a confused look. "We don't even know this guy and we're gonna drive with him for four hours?"

Mike had a slight buzz going and brushed it off, "We'll be fine. He's a good guy."

Ludwig said, "We should get on the road soon so we don't hit much traffic."

We finished our beers and got our things to head to Munich. An hour or so into our drive, we came to a dead stop because the autobahn, or highway, was closed off heading towards Munich. Ludwig cursed in German and told us we'd have to get off for a little bit otherwise we'd be sitting in this traffic for a couple hours, "So, let's go grab lunch."

We drove off the nearest exit to some small Bavarian village. Ludwig looked like a German Fabio and was so generous to us. Mike and I insisted on letting us grab lunch since he was giving us a ride. Ludwig refused, "What's the saying you Americans say… pay it forward?"

We smiled and thanked him a bunch of times. I was surprised us a complete stranger, his generosity towards us and I wondered to myself, *Why don't people do this more often?*

Munich was the city of Oktoberfest. Sadly, we were a little too early for that. The hostel we found had a big orange car with Jaegar drink label printed all over it. We didn't plan on staying long in Munich because Mike agreed to head to Austria with me so I could meet with Dominik.

When we arrived, we were welcomed with a free shot of Jaegar. If you don't know what it is, it's a black liquor that tastes like licorice; in other words, vomit central. After a combo of Jaegar and a long travel day, we went straight to bed and set up to have a tour to Dachau Concentration Camp. Mike said, "Yay, can't wait to be depressed tomorrow."

I'm a history buff and love to see historical places when I travel. I said, "It won't be that long and we'll just grab a beer after. I'm sure we'll need it."

Morning came and we dragged ourselves to breakfast in the common area that usually consisted of tea or coffee with a croissant for one or two euros, and met with our tour guide. Luckily, he was more chipper than we were and made the tour entertaining despite the solemn topic of our tour. As he introduced himself to the group, we slowly walked together to the gate where it said, "Arbeit Macht Frei," which translates to, "Work will set you free." Chills overwhelmed my body from the tips of me toes to my head as we all know that wasn't the case. My father, who is Argentinian, is also Jewish and to be on the grounds where so many other Jews perished was humbling.

It was a huge camp and a lot of it was taken down due to decay in the buildings. Fortunately, they remade a bunker for people to see where the prisoners lived. Everything was made of cheap wood. The beds were wooden without any mattresses or blankets. The tour guide continued to tell us stories as we walked through the bunkers. He mentioned that people who were in this camp knew the high probability of getting punished or tortured but never knew when. It's difficult to comprehend the psychological toll it must have been on people in Dachau. This particular concentration camp made it almost impossible to escape because guards were everywhere and they had guard towers with snipers who would kill anyone in a second if they even attempted to leave. They had an electric fence around the entire place so even if you tried you'd be electrocuted. I had a moment of, *What if this was my dad, my brother, and me in here?"* It brought tears to my eyes to even contemplate what people went through and to have witnessed their loved ones suffer.

To see this place first hand and run my fingers down the walls, to be able to walk into a cell and see the very same paint chipping off the walls will never leave me. Walking through crematoriums and gas chambers was enough to drain us for the rest of the day. Post concentration camp beers were a tranquil end to our day.

***

It had been about a month into our trip and Mike and I were spending 24/7 together. We began to clash. To save the rest of the trip from being an absolute disaster we started doing things on our own. We had *finally* made it to Austria. Salzburg is known as the city of salt and also the home of where the *Sound of Music* was filmed. I went on a city tour to see famous scenes from the movie and I asked to stop at this museum built into the mountain. I rode the elevator all the way to the top and saw the city, all the buildings were white like salt. A local came by and saw me taking in the sights and whispered, "*Salt is like gold here.*"

***

Mike and I met up to see the biggest ice cave in the world, also known as the 'World of Ice Giants.' We hiked for twenty minutes to reach the cable car that would take us the rest of the way up to the caves. As we rode the cable car, the view was spectacular, with luscious greenery as far as the eye could see. We were only dressed in light sweaters and pants and didn't realize how cold it would be to stand on the line even though was about eighty degrees down below where we hiked from. We slowly inched our way up the line close to the door where the tour guides waved us to come inside.

Once the door opened, it was like a vacuum of cold air literally sucked us into the cave. My shoes didn't have much of a grip, so I felt like I was being dragged in. The temperature was below freezing and we clearly missed the memo to bring something warm to wear. The formations were like stalactites and stalagmites but made completely with ice. I couldn't feel my fingers and toes by the end of the tour but the ice formations were worth it.

The tour guides would light pure magnesium as a source of light; it would burst into a bright white-ish light, Illuminating everything for a few moments before we'd all go into darkness until he lit another one and we were able to see again.

At the end of our tour, we rode the cable car down and gazed into the beauty of Austria. I drifted into dreamland of yearning to see Dominik again, especially since tomorrow would be the day, I'd be in Vienna like I promised him a year ago that I would. I still had his phone number printed on a small sheet of paper he gave me in the airport that I noticed only after unpacking my bag. He had stuffed it into one of my luggage pockets. I could see the numbers just well enough to make it out.

When we made back to our hostel, we found out that the hostel was big on the movie *The Sound of Music* and by that I mean, they played the movie 24/7 in their movie room. I'm not sure if that was a torture technique, but we checked out by the next morning. We booked a train ride straight to Vienna and I remembered Dominik told me to call him once I arrived.

Two hours or so later, we awoke from our half-assed naps, grabbed our packs, and found a hostel in the city. The hostel was tiny, hidden in the corner on a cobblestone street. It almost reminded me of a Sherlock Holmes film. The hostel was quaint and romantic and a perfect place to rest. Mike and I were still not on great terms. The hostel offered private rooms as well as dorm rooms. I chose to stay in a private room to give myself and Mike some alone time.

After I got settled into my room, I went to go find the nearest internet café to try and call Dominik and let him know that I was in town. I stood in the booth, nervously thinking, *What do I say? Will he remember me? Should I say Hello in German or English? What if he doesn't want to speak with me? What if he's not home?* I dialed the numbers with my heart in my throat and heard the ringtone. As I waited for him to answer, half wanting to hang up as I continued holding the phone, the phone started speaking in German, a message that I didn't understand. I tried again a few more times and the same thing happened. I opened the booth door and looked around for someone who hopefully spoke a little English to help me. I showed her the number I tried to call and what I pushed on the phone. She said, "Oh, you have to put the country code first and then try to dial."

She dialed for me and I knew soon he would be on the other end. A man with that slight British accent answered, and all I could say was, *"Hi, do you remember me?"* After I said that, I thought, *Good job, Laura, you didn't even say who you were. How is he going to know who this is asking do you remember me?*

He said, *"Of course, I remember you. My little Princess. Please tell me you're here in Vienna?"* My heart rose in excitement, partly relieved that he had remembered me.

"Where are you?" he asked. I told him where I was and he told me I wasn't far from the train station and mentioned which stop to get off. I was in disbelief that I was speaking to him again and I only made out, *"The third stop."* I assured him I would find it. I rode to where I thought he said, but it didn't look right. It looked like a bad area and I was confused because he never mentioned he lived in a bad area and said he was only a few stops from where my hostel was. The train conductor spoke over the speak first in German and then English, *"This is the last stop. Please transfer to your next train."*

Confused and worried that Dominik would think I stood him up, I found the train to go back to the main station and called him from there. "So, I'm guessing you're lost?" I laughed and apologized. Dominik told me the directions again and I paid more attention.

I found his stop. My heart and thoughts were racing, and butterflies filled my stomach. I quickly walked down the stairs to street level and there he was. That same sexy, messy hair, his smile that made me smile every time he looked at me. He was in the crowd of people waiting and he hadn't noticed me yet. I snuck around to surprise him. I slowly walked up to him and tapped his shoulder. He quickly turned around and picked me up in the biggest hug. "Oh, Laura, I've missed you! Come, my apartment is a short walk from here." Side by side, we held hands and walked to where Dominik lived. We both were in disbelief that I made it. I said, "Isn't it nice to not have to worry about Angela's angry glare?" Dominik laughed.

We were inseparable. His apartment was beautiful with big French windows, a bunk bed with only a top bunk and seating underneath. His room was simple with fresh white sheets and plump pillows. I said, "Oh you have a bunk bed! I'll just sleep up here."

Dominik said, "You're more than welcome to sleep next to me. But you may sleep wherever you wish." Young, naive and inexperienced, I tried to play it off and change topics. We talked for hours, reminiscing about our trip with People to People and how excited he was that I had made it to Vienna. I noticed a guitar leaning his wall. "Do you play the guitar?" Dominik picked it up and strummed the strings to tune it.

He said, "Please sit and enjoy as you will hear from the best guitar player in Vienna." I playfully rolled my eyes and obliged. He played nothing I could recognize as he went into a musical trance. I laid down on his couch as he continued to play, I could see the curtains flaring up as the wind blew in and I closed my eyes as I was being slowly serenaded. I awoke to him laying a small blanket over me as he sat next to me for a minute. I opened one eye and smiled.

Dominik said, "Rest if you want. I know you had a long travel day."

I said, "No, no, I was just relaxing. I'm just so hap..." Dominik leaned in and kissed me mid-sentence. I melted into him as I longed for us to kiss. I pulled back and whispered, "That I made it to Vienna." As I wanted to explore more of where this could go, I did not because mother nature had other plans.

Dominik wanted me to stay longer and go to The Netherlands with him and his friends to go camping the next morning. I knew Mike wouldn't be fond of me changing our plans and ditching him to go off with Dominik. Even though I secretly wanted to. Dominik and I enjoyed the very limited time we had to spend together.

***

Early the next morning, he made me a quick breakfast and then walked me to the train station back to my hostel. As we walked, I held back the tears because I didn't want to leave and wished we could have had more time. But once again, we had to part ways. I thought, *Why does it have to end? Why can't we make this work?* We stood in the middle of the underground of the train station. He caressed his hand against my cheek and gave me one last kiss.

I learned moments of love can last from a lifetime to a very short period of time. Any kind of love is worth the lesson. A part of me knew this wasn't going to work. We told each other we would keep in touch, but there was an awkward politeness where we both knew we were telling each other a white lie to soften the blow. He stayed in the middle of the station as I took the escalator to my train. I looked back at him watching me go up and gave him one last wave goodbye. I was beginning to learn nothing lasts forever and in traveling you have to get used to saying goodbye to people you meet.

Chapter 3: My Home Away from Home

2008

"Trust me, it's paradise. This is where the hungry come to feed. For mine is a generation that circles the globe and searches for something we haven't tried before. So never refuse an invitation, never resist the unfamiliar, never fail to be polite and never outstay the welcome. Just keep your mind open and suck in the experience. And if it hurts, you know? It's probably worth it." --The Beach, *Alex Garland*

Mike and I met back at our hostel to head to the train station to pick up our tickets to travel to Interlaken, Switzerland. The woman at the ticket window asked if we would like to upgrade our seats for a few more Euro. I thought being that it was a long overnight train, we would automatically get a sleeper car. Ten hours squished into a six-seater section, I wish we had upgraded our seats. Mike and I thought we had the car to ourselves and slowly more people came each time we stopped. There were six of us squished with our luggage on top of each other figuring out how to get comfortable and get some sleep.

After a while, the woman next to me asked if she could stretch her legs out over mine for a little bit. Hours of not being comfortable, I surrendered and asked as long as I can stretch my legs over hers as well. I only had a neck pillow and a light sweater to use as a blanket. I was able to finally fall asleep for a couple of hours and awoke to the train rocking back and forth. I opened one eye to see where we were and it was still dark outside. I saw the lady I put my legs on switched in a different position where her legs were straight up against the wall like an "L." I squinted my eyes at her in confusion as to how she was comfortable sleeping like that and went back to bed.

As the sun peeked through the window illuminating where we slept, I took off my hood that I was using as a makeshift eye mask, rubbed my eyes, and saw nothing but the beautiful Swiss Alps. I saw Mike was already awake and whispered, "Are we in Interlaken?" He said, "Yeah, it's the next stop." After being completely exhausted from our train ride, we wanted to find our hostel. We looked for the tourist section in the train station for local hostels and saw one for,

'The Funny Farm.' We chose that hostel because it made us laugh. The hostel had a plethora of adventurous activities to do, including hang gliding, skydiving, bungee jumping, white water rafting, to name a few.

The first guy we met was outside hanging around the bonfire. I will never forget his name, Noodle, he introduced himself along with his South Korean friend, Sam, who barely spoke a word of English; they had just met a few hours ago.

***

We grabbed some beers at the poolside bar and thought about going for a swim. The weather was kind of shitty and I knew I wasn't going in, but Sam and Noodle decided they *were* going in. I had to get this on camera. Noodle tackled Sam right into the pool and Sam screeched the girliest yelp I'd ever heard, and we were all laughing so hard tears were streaming down our faces. I loved this hostel already. The views were spectacular and The Jungfrau was the most gorgeous mountain I've ever seen, with the snowcaps still visible on its peaks. We met most of the staff at The Funny Farm and they were the most welcoming people.

I noticed a big yellow and red spiral painted at the bottom of the pool, and I asked one of the guys who worked at Alpin Raft, the activities company, if that meant anything. He said, "Be careful staying here at The Funny Farm, people get stuck here and never want to leave." That struck me, and I felt at home in weird way. There was something about it. It was a place where no matter who you are or where you come from, you were accepted.

The community of strangers at the hostel in a short period of time became friends, exchanging, *"Where are you from? What's your story? How long have you traveled?"* Everyone had a story. I became curious and intrigued by everyone I met. I would have some of the deepest conversations with some of these people who were strangers than with friends I had back home. I noticed people let their walls down. They were more open to talking and getting to know you, whereas back home you could walk down the street without having someone say hello or even a smile.

Our first adventurous activity was hang-gliding with Hang Gliding Interlaken. We met our guides at the front of the main hotel, The Mattenhof, to get our gear ready and sign our waiver forms. Our guides introduced themselves, Greg and

James. James was this ballsy high energy Aussie. I immediately loved his energy because he got me excited about the activity. James said, "I'm the crazy one, who wants to ride with me?" Mike was quiet and hungover from the night before.

I said, "I'm down for it!" We drove twenty minutes up a mountain where we would be taking off. The view from the take off point was beautiful. Jungfrau was in the background along with the town of Interlaken, which looked impossibly tiny from where I was standing. Greg and James told us to enjoy the view for a little bit as they set up the gliders. Mike and I went to the edge of the cliff to see all of Interlaken below. I said, "Isn't this so fucking beautiful?" Mike shook his head in agreement. I shook him a little to get him excited and said, "Come on, get pumped! We're about to fly over that!"

Mike laughed and said, "I am, I'm just dying a little bit. And I'm hoping I don't puke." I shook my head, chuckled, and said, "Good luck with that."

Greg and James walked over to set us up in gear. We wore what looked like a baseball catcher's outfit but it went from the front top of the shoulders all the way down to our feet, which would hold us in the glider like a hammock. James had fun bright colored helmets with stars on them. He put the helmet on me to make sure it was on correctly. I looked over at Mike and he was geared up and ready to go. James asked if I wanted to go first or second. I said, "Let's go first."

James pulled me to the side with my gear on and explained the running we'd have to do together and holding on to his shoulder strap. "It goes like this, step, step, run, run." We practiced a few times and then walked to the edge of the mountain.

James asked, "Are you nervous?"

I said, "A little."

He said, "Okay, well make sure you run with me because if we don't get enough speed then we don't get enough air and then we'll crash and die."

I laughed nervously, "Well, that's good to know."

"Are you ready?" A rush of adrenaline overcame my body as we did 'step, step, run, run' down a little path off the mountain and we took flight.

The view from flying above the lake with the Alps in the background was breathtakingly beautiful. James mounted a camera on his glider that was placed on a long metal rod to take pictures of us. I was mesmerized by the scenery, and to James' surprise I was unusually quiet. James, being ballsy, asked if I liked roller coasters. I said that I did and snapped me back to reality when all of a sudden, I couldn't figure out what was going on or which direction we were flying in, but we did a vertical nose dive and then he took a picture of the priceless look on my face.

When we landed, I saw Mike walk off for a few minutes. I told James he probably shouldn't have drank the night before going hang gliding. James laughed and shook his head and screamed out, *"You alright mate!"* Mike waved at us in assurance that he'll be fine.

When we arrived back at the Funny Farm, we decided to check out and catch a break from all the partying to visit Grindelwald, which is a town surrounded by the Alps. We stayed at The Mountain Hostel, which was smack in the middle of the valley. From the partying to the dead silence of the mountains was a big change. The rules were lame and there wasn't much to do.

I rode a cable car up to the top of the mountain, which happened to be the longest cable car ride in Europe. There were cows all along the mountain sides grazing. All I heard were bells--that's when you know you are in Switzerland.

After a few days of too much quiet we went back to the Funny Farm. They immediately remembered us; being at this hostel felt like coming home to family. Mike and I became close with the staff, and I told the manager Luca, "I will come back and work here one day." He said, "Become a European citizen and you'll have a job waiting for you."

***

Matteo was the full of life Italian with a contagious laugh who always knew how to have a good time. We initially met at the bar a few times while he was working but didn't have a chance to speak other than the occasional hello. In the back of the hostel, where the backpackers stayed, they called it the barn probably we were a bunch of wild animals partying. The barn had shared bathrooms and showers. You had to walk out of the building where our rooms were, go outside and walk back in another door below to find the showers. Matteo and I bumped into each other a few times inside washing our hands. After the third time, he said, *"Oh, it's you again."* I smiled and we shook hands to officially introduce ourselves. He winked and said, "I guess I'll see you around."

I walked out to hit up the space tent, which was an area near the pool that had bench tables under a big white tent and a big red gondola car as the kitchen to serve burgers and drinks. A sweet woman who introduced herself to me as Nina became my sister away from home while I stayed at The Funny Farm. She was known as Nina, 'The Burger Queen' because she made the best burgers. She and I hit it off and she told me to wait around because her shift was almost finished. She offered to go grab drinks at The Caverne, the club underneath The Mattenhof. It was nothing special, a small space packed with cheesy decorations, amateur lighting and sound systems filled with Swissys and backpackers. No one took it too seriously, but everyone was there to have a good time.

I asked if Matteo was still working. She said, "He's done for the day but he's probably home. Want me to invite him out with us?"

I nodded my head, "Yeah, bring his ass out with us." Nina and I had a few more drinks down in the Caverne waiting for Matteo. A few moments later, he strolled in. He came and put his arms around me twirling my hair and said to Nina, *"Do you see how gorgeous this girl is?"* She laughed and said, "Take it easy with her, she's a good one." I was magnetized to his infectious energy and we were glued to each other all night dancing and laughing. In the midst of us dancing the night away, he dipped me and kissed me. He whispered, "Let's go take a walk outside for some fresh air."

We headed down the street to another hostel that had an underground club and we stayed to have more drinks but the music wasn't good so we walked back five minutes down the road back to the Mattenhof to hang out in the lobby. The lights were off and the lobby bar was closed for the night but Matteo was screaming, *"SHOTS!"* which echoed throughout the lobby. I covered his mouth to mask the noise so we wouldn't get in trouble. The two of us kept bumping into things and laughing incessantly. Matteo then broke a shot glass on the floor. Nina came running in and said, "Mike drank too much and is sick; you may want to go look after him." I stumbled my way over to Matteo to say goodnight. *"Goodnight beautiful, see you tomorrow."*

I went to Mike to see if he was okay. He was by the poolside puking into a trashcan. I said, "You good?" He mumbled and shook his head up and down. I went to grab water from the space tent bar and handed it to him. "Here take some water and let's bring you to bed, just hold on to me." I said. Mike and I both struggled and stumbled our way to our dorm. I left a can next to Mike's bed just in a case and crawled into bed. We both didn't wake up until the afternoon the next day. I usually awoke first because I always needed food after a night of drinking. I walked outside our dorm room downstairs, outside and back inside below to use the sink to brush my teeth. When I went back upstairs, my key wouldn't work. I didn't want to wake anyone up and I had to go to the front desk to reactivate my card. I had been at The Funny Farm for about two weeks, and after a certain point the card deactivates.

The woman at the front desk took my card and introduced herself, "I'm Verena, seems like you've been here a long time?"

I giggled and said, "Nice to meet you, and yes I don't think my cousin and I are going to leave anytime soon."

She had an intense presence and she asked a lot of questions of where I was from, who I knew around here, if I'd made any friends yet, who I was hanging out with, and so on. With a slightly uncomfortable look on my face, I answered her questions quickly and said, "Ok, I have to go now. See you around."

I went back to my room and the key worked. I grabbed some of my things and went to the COOP, a local grocery store, to grab a few things to eat. I then walked to the poolside and found Mike recovering from the night before. I pulled up a chair and both of us sat there experiencing the meanest hangover yet completely zoned out. I said, "What are we going to do today?"

Mike put his head in hands and softly said, "I don't know."

Some of the staff from Alpin Raft saw us struggling and were looking for people to come canyoning. They came to our table, sat for a moment, and said, "Rough night, huh? Come canyoning with us."

I said, "What the hell is that? We're so hungover."

One of them said, "Oh, it's a blast. Canyoning is the best cure for hangovers."

We overheard the table next to us talking about canyoning. It's hiking through a canyon that has natural waterslides and cliffs to jump from. Mike and I thought, "*Eh, why not?*" Perhaps we were ballsy and maybe a little cocky too, so we chose the most hardcore one, which was seven hours long in one of their biggest canyons.

We met at the Alpin Raft headquarters, which was right near our dorm room building. We picked up our wetsuits and helmets. Each helmet had nicknames painted on the front so the guides can call you by your nickname. It was easier than remembering everyone's name. I closed my eyes and dropped my hand into the bucket filled with helmets and grabbed one that said in big, fat letters, 'TWAT.' Mike died of laughter.

I said, "There's no fucking way I'm being called a Twat all day." I picked another one without looking that said, 'Amore' – much better. The guides gave us a pre-canyoning beer to start the mood off right.

We got on the bus to head to the hike in. The guides were on the bus with us hyping up the group, which only made it more exciting. Twenty minutes later we arrived. We all were in our wetsuits and had to hike into the canyon. It was quite a hike, which I didn't expect. Hiking in a tight wetsuit in hot weather was like being wrapped in plastic wrap. I wanted to get to the canyon already. Eventually, we got there and the guides sat the group of us in a circle to tell us the rules. "1. Always listen to your guide. 2. Have fun 3. Look out for each other. 4. Always listen to your guide." We couldn't bitch out deeper inside the canyon because the only way out was by helicopter and that's only if we broke a leg or something worse. I was growing a little apprehensive as I had zero clue what this involved.

Finn was one of the guides. He had salt and pepper colored hair with a gnarly goatee. Introducing himself, he said, "I'm the crazy Kiwi from New Zealand." With him, I knew we were in for a wild ride. We met plenty of Kiwis at the hostel and they all were nuts but in the best kind of way. Adrenaline junkies, mostly. There were about ten to fifteen of us and I was the only girl in the group. Finn told us about a recent story where a group died in the canyon due to a flash flood and then said, "Alright, let's go!" My heart was pounding out of my chest with a mixture of adrenaline and nerves. A part of me wanted to leave but I felt like I had no choice but to follow everyone.

***

After hiking in deeper into the canyon, I broke a sweat. We arrived at a small pool of water that we had to walk into in order to get to the other side of the trail. I didn't anticipate the water being as cold as it was, especially since we were in the middle of summer. *(We were in Switzerland, duh. And this was glacier water)*. When my body hit the water, I started hyperventilating from the cold. I didn't realize my wetsuit had not been zipped up all the way, and the water went down into my suit. I was caught off guard and freaked out a little, and then I noticed immediately on the other side of the trail was a 30ft jump. I'm not normally afraid of heights, but the other guide, Nico, said, "Make sure you jump into that little spot because to the left is a huge rock and you could break your leg." I thought, *Holy fuck, I have to jump in the 'right' spot?!* I said, "No way!" Nico said in disappointment, "I thought you weren't afraid of heights."

I said, "Yeah, but this is fucking high, dude." Nico seemed bummed I wouldn't do it, but he rappelled me down the side of the rock to the bottom and I watched everyone else jump. I wanted to quit. I was not enjoying this and we had only just started. We didn't have much protective gear other than a plastic helmet and a life vest, but we also had a rubber mat on our butts that made us go down the slides even faster. I didn't realize how dangerous canyoning was. The slides were the worst. They were like nature's version of the slip and slide. The currents were so powerful, I felt like I was not in control. Finn flew down the slides like it was nothing. I thought he was out of his mind.

We walked through the water to the first slide after watching Finn go down first to show everyone how to properly slide down. Nico was at the top helping people position themselves to slide down. I let a few people go ahead of me because I was terrified. Now it was my turn. I dragged myself to the edge of the slide. Nico told me to lie down and stick my left arm out and hold it there so I didn't turn over. It was a vertical drop to the bottom into a pool of water. I took a breath and Nico said, "Ready?" Before I could answer, he let me go. I closed my eyes tightly shut, zoomed down, and the current from the water hit my face so hard I thought I had broken my nose. *I wanted out.*

Finn was laughing once I hit the pool of water. "Did you enjoy that?"

"Nope, not at all." I said.

Next, we had to all swim underneath a waterfall to get to the other side. It was difficult to try to dive with our life vests on and some people in the group got stuck underneath the waterfall for a few seconds before popping up on the other side. The next jump was called the 'Bonsai' jump – a slide that shot off the edge of a waterfall, and on the way down, the guides told us we have to scream *'BONSAI!'* I was at the top with Finn and I told him I couldn't do it.

He said, "Yes you can."

A bunch of others went before me and they were all cheering me on from the bottom. I was scared shitless but I did it and when I went to scream the word 'BONSAI,' all I got out was "BON" and the rest was a high-pitched scream. When I swam up, all the guys were laughing so hard because I barely got the word bonsai out. I laughed along with them, but secretly wanted to cry because I couldn't take this anymore. As we swam up on dryer parts of the canyon, Nico led the front and Finn was in the back. Nico yelled out, "Hold the person in front of you, there's a little string on each of your life vests because this next part is slippery and very narrow." We all slowly walked on the edge of the canyon rock that was no bigger than a couple inches, holding onto the string of the person in front of us so no one would fall. We had water shoes on but some of the rocks had algae that made it extremely slippery.

Nico yelled out, "Okay, now we're here at the 'Matrix' jump. Have we all seen the Matrix?" A majority of us raised our hands. "Well, the infamous Matrix jump will be needed for this next one. Please watch as I demonstrate and be aware there are photographers in the woods to take the best jump shot." Finn told the group to back up slowly to give Nico some room to demonstrate. Nico somehow ran along the couple inches of rock and kicked off a slanted wall to emulate the Matrix jump from the movie into a pool of water. The guys ahead of me tried. Some failed miserably, but others did it. I ran up and kicked off the wall and did the jump quite well. The guys cheered as I hit the water. I enjoyed that jump because I didn't feel like I was going to die. Mike said, "One more jump and we're done." To try to ease my utter discomfort.

The big finale was another high jump and since I didn't do the first one, I felt obligated to jump this one and it was higher than the first. We all had to climb up to the top of the cliff. The guides told us we could do any kind of jump we wanted. The photographers were staged perfectly in front of the cliff to take a picture of our jump.

Again, I let a few people go ahead of me to mentally prepare. A few guys jumped with no problem. Mike was up next. He tried to do a cool jump by kicking out mid-air but didn't position himself in time as he hit the water and landed on his back. Everyone gasped, "Oh shit!" I walked to the edge and we were yelling at Mike to see if he was alright. He didn't respond for a few seconds. I yelled to Finn, "Finn! Go grab Mike!" By the time Finn jumped in, Mike slowly started moving around and waved to say he was fine. He couldn't speak because he got the wind knocked out of him. I was relieved he was okay. Now I was extra nervous. Nico was at the top encouraging everyone.

I walked up to Nico, he smiled and said, "Oh you're actually gonna jump now?"

I took a deep regretful breath, "Yeah, I guess so."

Nico counted 1,2,3 in German. "Eins, Zwei, Drei!" And I jumped off. In mid-air I thought to myself, *Holy shit, I'm still falling!* that's how high it was. I joined the group and we waited for the rest of the people to jump. Once everyone was accounted for, we hiked up to a small open area that had a few benches to sit and relax. Finn and Nico brought Swiss cheeses, meats and beers. Finn and Nico raised their beers, "Thank you all for coming out. I'm glad everyone made it alive. Cheers!"

Finn saw me, smiled, and walked over. "So are you happy you did it or that it's over?"

I chuckled, "That it's over."

Finn hugged me from the side and said, "You did good, kid."

We hiked out of the woods and the bus was waiting for us at the bottom of the canyon. Prior to getting on the bus, Nico told us they were going to take some group shots. The first one, Finn said, "Okay, everyone let's do the wave at the camera pose." We all put our hands up to wave and smile at the camera. "Now, let's do a fuck yeah, rock and roll pose." Everyone did their best rock and roll impression to the camera. It was 2008 at the time and George Bush was still President, which explains this next one. "So last one, since everyone hates George Bush, let's give the middle finger to the camera." We all laughed and gave the finger to the camera. Nico and Finn told us we'd get the photos when we headed back to headquarters.

***

We piled on the bus with our gear still on. Everyone was obliterated and once the bus turned on and started driving, I was knocked out. When we got back to The Funny Farm in the afternoon, Mike and I went straight to bed. We didn't wake up until 11:00 p.m. later that night. We ventured outside to see what people and the staff were up to. "Did you guys just wake up?" said Matteo.

I mumbled, "Yeah," as I yawned and asked for a beer for Mike and myself. I joked and said, "We have the canyoning hangover."

Matteo shook his head in agreement and said, "Yup, it's no joke. Get a good night's rest because tomorrow is Swiss National Day and there's going to be a big party." Matteo was in charge of setting up the parties around the hostel. They were always wild and a lot of fun. We finished our beers and said goodbye to Matteo then went back to bed for an early night.

We had our first restful night sleep in a long time. We'd been at The Funny Farm about two and a half weeks now. There was nothing that could get us to leave this place. Any good night sleep was a Godsend from all the activities and partying. Swiss National is one of their biggest parties, think of it as America's Fourth of July. Everyone dressed up patriotically, there are drinks, barbeques, and of course, fireworks. In the middle of Interlaken there's a huge field where all the hang gliders and paragliders land. They have huge life-sized letters to spell out 'INTERLAKEN.' We heard that's where they do an awesome firework show.

Mike and I walked over to Space Camp to say hi to Nina and keep her company. "How was canyoning?"

"It was fun, scary, and exhausting," I said. She asked if we wanted a beer.

We said no, so we could prepare for later, but Mike said, "We'll have your famous burgers though."

Matteo and another bartender came around the corner to hang out and chat with us. Matteo, of course, started pouring shots. "Jesus Christ, we can't get away from you with the shots, can we?" I said. But we couldn't refuse the invitation. Two weeks felt like two years being with all these people. I mean that sincerely. They took me and my cousin in and made us a part of the crew. It was surreal to be surrounded by the purest form of love from people we had only just met.

We picked up our tiny shot glasses and in Funny Farm or Swiss style, I'm not sure, they showed us to hold the shot with our pinky finger on the bottom and our thumb on the top. We all simultaneously yelled, *"Oooooyyyy!"* and then took the shot. Thinking of that moment still sends chills over my body. It hit me how much I loved these people, Switzerland, and especially The Funny Farm.

Matteo and I ordered our beers and were beginning to get drunk, just laughing and chatting with the other backpackers. He said, "Just wait till you see the Caverne during today because of the holiday, it's a lot more fun." The other bartenders were holding a contest to win a whole bottle of Jager by playing a game of volleyball at the Guinness tent, which was another outdoor bar. Most of us would go to the Guinness tent once the bar at Space Camp closed then after that people moved to the club Caverne at the main hotel. There was a section behind the bar that had a bonfire pit and benches for people to sit, drink, and chat. In front of the Guinness tent they had a sand pit with a legit volleyball net. Mike and some backpackers he met at the bar were a team.

I scoffed, "They're going to lose, they're already drunk." A couple backpackers sitting next to me started to laugh. As I predicted, Mike's team lost. It was brutal to watch.

Mike said, "Ehh, shit happens. Let's go watch the fireworks in town." We found some bikes lying around. Tipsy bike riding isn't easy but we somehow made it to town. There was a big crowd already filling the street. They began setting off the fireworks behind the big 'Interlaken' letters and it was awesome.

I asked Mike, "What do you want to do after this?" Mike wasn't sure, but I suggested hitting up the Caverne since Matteo said it would be good tonight. Mike and I grabbed our bikes and rode back to The Mattenhof. We saw some people already heading down towards the club. We parked our bikes in the back and walked to the club. The DJ sounded amazing from the outside as we waited on the line.

***

Matteo and Nina came down shortly after. Mike and I bought them a round of beers, but Matteo insisted on buying my drink. Mike was getting pissed off that he was spending so much money on beer and I wasn't. I said in a cheeky attitude, "I can't help that guys want to buy me drinks." Caverne was getting so packed with people that it was hard to move. It's a small club so it was unbearably hot. Matteo mouthed to me, "Do you want to go outside?" and pointed out at the door. I saw that Mike was with Nina having a good time and I left with Matteo.

We went outside so he could smoke a spliff. He offered it to me but I was too hot and tipsy. The moon was gorgeous over the Jungfrau. There was a slight chill in the air, and Matteo was moving closer to me to get warm. We started talking about life, Italy, and why he left. He took a deep inhale of his spliff and blew out a cloud of smoke.

He looked over at me and leaned in for a kiss. The last guy I had kissed was Dominik back in Vienna and I thought of him for a split second because I realized I had forgotten about him. He never reached back out to me since I left. Matteo invited me back to his place. We took a five or ten minute cab ride to a small town nearby. It was dark, so I couldn't see the outside of his home very well but when we walked inside, he had a postcard view of the Swiss Alps. He turned on the lights and there were exposed wooden beams in the ceiling. It was beautiful. Matteo asked if I wanted another drink. I said, "No, no thanks. I'm already pretty tipsy from the bar." I remember chatting with my friend, Emma, who I was still in touch with from People to People a few days prior, asking her about sex and what it felt like. Emma said it felt wonderful. I said, "No Emma, like, what does it really feel like? What can you compare it to?"

Emma giggled, "Hmm let me think. Well, I guess it's kind of like a big tampon." I laughed but I guess I had somewhat of an idea what to expect. Matteo and I began kissing passionately and our clothes were starting to come off. When I knew in my mind this was going to happen, I relaxed my body and went with the flow. The moment where I was no longer a virgin, I thought, *This is it?* I expected pain or sparks to fly from what other girls have told me, but my first time was sensual and gentle. I didn't want to tell Matteo that I was a virgin and potentially judge me for any possible reason, so I kept that little secret to myself. As we laid in bed, Matteo was looking at me as he ran his fingers through my hair. "This means so much more to me."

I said, "What does?"

"All of this, everything with you." I smiled and kissed him.

"Let's go to bed," Matteo suggested.

The next morning, I woke up with a mean hangover. I looked at the time and thought, "Shit, it's noon already?" Matteo wasn't next to me but he heard me ruffling the covers around and opened the door with a wooden tray with some toast and jam and a cup of tea.

He said, "Please eat something. I'm going to shower and we'll take the bus back together to The Funny Farm."

I was falling for Matteo. I loved his full of life energy, and perhaps I felt a little bit jealous that I didn't have an ounce of what he had. Being around him brought it out of me. We walked to the bus stop and headed back to the hostel. He had to do some work at the Mattenhof today and I just wanted to shower and go back to bed. I was wearing one of his shirts and he stopped at the bottom of the steps to go inside. "Kiss me," he said.

We kissed and I said, "I'll see you around later."

I decided to lounge by the pool the rest of the day instead to write in my travel journal. Verena saw me laying out and come over to say hi. She sat down next to me, trying to peek over to see what I was writing. I closed my book and said, "What's up?"

She said with a sly tone, "I know who you like."

"I don't like anyone." I said I don't because everyone talks around here and she would be the last person I'd tell who I liked. Even though I denied it. I knew she knew and she knew I was lying. She tried to pawn me off and mentioned the new DJ they just hired had a big crush on me. I wasn't attracted to him, but I knew what she was up to and I assumed she probably liked Matteo too. I tried my best to give her the shortest answers to give her the impression to fuck off. Eventually, she understood and walked to Space Camp where the others were.

Nina then came over to me because she saw Verena sitting with me. "Everything alright, love?" I explained that I was a little annoyed by Verena coming over questioning me about who I liked around here and told her my assumption is that she knows I like Matteo.

Nina said, "This is a small town, I don't doubt she knows. Plus, Matteo is a good guy. People are noticing because he likes you a lot and we've never seen him like this with a girl like how he is with you."

***

It was getting warmer out. I told Nina to come in for a swim. She didn't have her swimsuit and said she'd go home quickly and grab it. I hopped into the water to cool off and swam up on a big lounging raft. I floated around the pool and relaxed until both Verena and Matteo jumped on with me. I screamed, "What the fuck? You guys scared me!" Verena was being flirtatious to make sure I noticed with Matteo but what surprised me was, Matteo was flirting back. I was pissed off but tried to hide it and got off the raft to swim elsewhere. Nina came back and I just looked at her and she knew.

She looked at me and mouthed, "Ignore her."

I got out of the pool to warm up again and tan by the poolside and Nina laid out a big towel to lay on. I said, "Let me grab us some fries to share and beers." Whenever you ordered something at Space Camp, they would scream your name across the pool, and most of the time it was embarrassingly loud. Ten or so minutes later, *"LAURA!!"*

I ran up and grabbed our food and drinks as fast as I could. Nina and I sat there watching Verena and Matteo swim together in the pool. I whispered to her, "I'm so confused as to what's going on." Nina just shook her head and agreed.

Nina asked, "Did you guys hook up last night?"

I told her yeah but I did not tell her it was my first time. Verena got out of the pool and saw Nina sitting with me. She came over to say hi to Nina. Verena asked me, "Do I piss you off?" Nina told her to piss off and leave me alone.

I said, "She's brutal, huh? She just doesn't stop." She immediately went to Matteo and was all over him in clear sight of me seeing them both. Matteo was enjoying it, too. I didn't play into her games and I didn't want her or Matteo to know or see that it was bothering me. I pretended I didn't care and went off to hang out at the Guinness tent away from them.

By the time night rolled around, Matteo, Verena, Nina, Mike, and myself were all wasted. I admit we were a bit like alcoholics that summer. Anyway, everything else closed and soon Caverne was opening. We all wanted to have one more night out together despite the tension because soon I'd have to leave back to the states. Mike decided to stay longer but I was going to head home because my money was running out. One last hoorah and after about twenty days at The Funny Farm it was time to part ways. We were all dancing the night away, it was like a party just for me and Mike. The DJ even shouted us out, "Let's all cheer to Laura and Mike as they have become members of The Funny Farm family!" Everyone was cheering and raising their glasses.

Out of the corner of my eye, I could see Matteo kissing Verena all over her neck. That was enough for me. I left my full drink and walked out. Nina came after me. I walked outside to get some fresh air and Nina said, "Why did you leave?" I just bawled.

Nina immediately hugged me and said, "Oh sweetie, please don't cry. Is it about Matteo and Verena?"

I said, "Yeah, why is he such an asshole? I thought he actually liked me."

"I thought so too," said Nina. Nina wiped my tears and I said, "You feel like my sister and even though I'm really upset, I'm glad you're here." Nina hugged me tight to ease my pain. Matteo walked out and sat on the stairs not too far away from us to smoke a spliff. I wiped my tears and went up to his face, "So, you like Verena? You said you liked me. You're such an asshole. Fuck you, Matteo."

Matteo shot right back, "Fuck you, too."

"No, FUCK YOU! You're such a jerk," as I got more into his face. "Call yourself a taxi and go home. No one wants you here. Leave! Just go!"

Nina grabbed me and walked me away from him. "He's being a dick right now. I don't understand why he's doing this to you. We're all drunk, let's just get you home. Let it be for now. You leave tomorrow anyway."

With barely any sleep, I packed my things, said bye to Mike and told him to be safe and let me know when he heads back home and then I made my way to the lobby. I had to catch my train at noon and I wanted to say my goodbyes. I said goodbye to Luca and he said, "You'll have a job here, just get that EU passport."

Nina was just walking in and I ran up to her and gave her a big hug. We were both crying and she said, "Are you sure you want to leave?" My heart didn't want to leave but I felt like I had to get back home. Plus, I didn't have much money left. I felt like I left a piece of my heart in Interlaken. And Matteo? Well, we never got to say goodbye. Staying at The Funny Farm was a huge learning experience for me. Did I get hurt in the end? Yes. But you know what? It was worth it.

Chapter 4: Dear Xanax, It's Over.

2009

"Sometimes it takes great suffering to pierce the soul and open it up to greatness"

-Jocelyn Murray

I wouldn't ever have expected the emotional pain I was going to endure for the next five plus years. I was in school at John Jay College of Criminal Justice studying to get my B.A. degree in Forensic Psychology. I was currently studying drug use and abuse during my semester, and I was just finishing reading up on overdosing. I came home, and my dad told me that my brother, Steven, didn't look right. I wasn't initially alarmed, but I walked upstairs to my room and peeked in his room. I saw him sitting up on the bed with a glazed look in his eyes and pale skin. I asked what was wrong, and he didn't say anything. I knew from what I studied earlier in the day that he was overdosing. I told my dad to call 9-1-1 immediately. I noticed circular burn marks on Steven's wrists. They were cigarette burns.

The paramedics arrived. I knew one of them from high school (and I was embarrassed) of the circumstances. The paramedics asked if my brother had taken anything. Steven admitted he took a lot of over the counter pills and alcohol. The paramedic continued to question him and then asked, "Did you do this on purpose? Are you feeling suicidal right now?" My brother answered, "Yes" to both questions.

Everything in the room became muffled. My mind was observing all of this in slow motion. I couldn't wrap my head around what Steven had just said. *My little brother wants to die?*

I felt like I blacked out. After the paramedics took him to the hospital, my dad accompanied him and told me to stay home and come in the morning. I shut my door and with my hands shaking, my voice trembling, I called my sister and mom to let them know what had happened. I had never cried harder in my life. I felt like a piece of my soul had died.

Visiting my brother in a psych ward was strange and surreal. I was heartbroken my own brother was in there alone. It killed me to leave him there. I felt like I needed to protect him. Ever since we were little I felt a strong connection with my brother, as if maybe we were brother and sister in another life. When kids in the older class would bully him because he was smaller than the rest, I was there to take the heat and yell at whoever bothered him. I remember when a kid threw sand in my brother's eye at the playground. My brother started crying, and the teachers didn't help, but I was there using my little fingers to brush the sand off his face, away from his eyes.

When I went to visit my brother in the hospital, the look on my dad's face broke my heart. I can't imagine what it feels like to be a parent and see your child go through pain so intense that they don't want to live anymore. There is a grieving process humans go through when we experience trauma. Shock, anger, sadness. I was unbelievably angry with Steven, and yet I was incredibly sad at the same time.

This went on for years… more suicide attempts, more drunken antics, and gut-wrenching worry. I felt my brother's pain and I felt helpless. I couldn't protect him. Only later on would I understand it wasn't my responsibility to protect him. None of us truly would understand what his issues are. We knew he was depressed but he wouldn't say why. Even today, we don't truly know what the issue stems from.

I began losing myself. Nights I'd go to sleep, my brother would come home in the middle of the night drunk struggling to come up the stairs loudly with his heavy feet. My heart would be racing, I'd wait till he went to bed, and I'd go into his room to check on him and make sure he was breathing. I'd wait until I saw his chest rise and then go back to bed. I did this almost every night he came home. This is where my anxiety took hold of my body. I made the smart choice after these series of events to go right into therapy.

I had this wonderful therapist named Mitchell, who was this tiny guy who had a 'give it to ya straight' attitude but was balanced with empathy when it was needed. I saw him twice a week every week, and I'd go there crying beyond belief. Old feelings from my childhood came up along with the open wound in my heart of my brother. He recommended I go on medications to ease my anxiety and panic attacks in order to heal through this process. I was against medications, but felt like I didn't have any other option at the time. I was on Zoloft and Prozac and I carried Xanax with me for emergencies. I was a zombie. But I didn't give a fuck.

Antidepressants are good at making you feel numb. I dealt with panic attacks and anxiety daily, and working towards getting my B.A. degree was wearing on me, too. It even got to a point where I didn't leave my house for a month and I stopped hanging out with my friends because I was too anxious to be in social settings.

Mitchell quit. And I felt like a piece of my soul died, again. I called Mitchell upset about him not telling me and he deeply apologized that the office didn't call me. He was moving back to Brooklyn and would be out of my network. I sat in my car and cried my eyes out after I got off the phone with him. *Why did he have to leave? This isn't fair. Maybe this is a sign.* As upset as I was, I tried to see what this could possibly mean for me. I was in the deepest turmoil I've ever been in and I had no choice but to try to see the light.

The antidepressants did help me during therapy, but after two or so years, it began to wear on me. I would come home after school and go right to my psychiatrist. I'd sit in that waiting room for sometimes three hours to then only talk to the doctor for five minutes. The psychiatrists didn't care about how you were feeling--at least they didn't make it seem that way. I'd cry for five minutes, and they'd write me a script.

During one of my sessions with a psychiatrist, I had a moment of epiphany. Everything became clear again, and I noticed as I was crying my fears and pain to this man, he did not look at me once. He wrote notes in his notepad and then switched to write out scripts for me. I stopped talking for a moment to see if he would even notice. It took him a few minutes and I said, "You really don't give a shit, do you?" Not that I was ever suicidal ever, but I was trying to make my point so I said, "If I jumped off a bridge after this you wouldn't give two shits about me." He was taken aback by what I was saying and said that wasn't true. I said, "It's all about the money for you. You just write your scripts and get your money." He said it wasn't about the money but based on the energy he was giving off since I was seeing him, it was.

***

I was raising my voice at this point, and I said, "You money hungry mother fucker." And I told him I didn't want to be on medications anymore. I continued to say to him, "If I want to cry then I want to cry. If I'm angry then I want to be angry. I want to feel my emotions again without feeling guilty for them."

I walked out of the session and went to my car filled with adrenaline, filled with emotion I hadn't felt in a long time after being so numb on medications. I cried. I called my sister and told her what happened, and she let me vent. Not much longer after I called my psychiatrist, I said I wanted to go off of Prozac. When the male psychiatrist wasn't there, a woman took his place. She thought it wasn't a good idea at first, but I said no I'm done, I want to *feel* again. She said she would wean me off slowly. Mind you, I was scared shitless to come off my meds, as they had become my crutch. I still had my Xanax on me but I stopped taking it. I wanted to work through my emotions without drugs, no matter how hard or scary it was. I missed being myself and mostly being clear-headed.

I began seeing a new therapist, who was more spiritual. She was into yoga and meditation. I remember one session with her in particular where I was having an anxiety attack in her office. She immediately guided me into a meditation. She told me to go to a place where I felt calm and at ease. In my mind I went back to a place in Canada where my dad, my brother, and I have visited since I was little. It was in the middle of nowhere, where we stayed in shitty cabins along a lake and went fishing for a week. There was no TV, no internet, and no phone service, and it was all about being around nature and enjoying family. My mind went to me sitting on the docks being gently rocked back and forth as small waves moved under the docks and boats drove by. My body immediately felt calm. I went to a place where I felt safe and comfortable. I realized the anxiety was no longer there.

Chapter 5: Leap, and The World Will Throw You a Net

2013

"You are what you love, not what loves you."--Adaptation

In the midst of coming off my meds and trying to get myself back on my feet emotionally and spiritually, I began reading books on self-development and Buddhism to learn how to calm my mind. I met this girl through my travel blog who had just attended to a seminar in Los Angeles hosted by a guy who is a comedian turned transformational speaker. I had zero clue what it was about, but she said he recently dealt with anxiety to the point of wanting to end his life but overcame it in three months. I was in a place of feeling completely lost and not knowing which direction to go, but I decided to reach out to her friend, Kyle Cease, myself and tell him I was interested in going to his event in LA. I didn't think he would get back to me, but Kyle immediately wrote back to me saying he was expecting to hear from me. Kyle gave me his program at the time called, "Panic Free Life." He said, "I will give you this one for free. Try it out and see how you feel afterwards."

Despite my anxiety, I am a motivated and driven person; when I set my mind to something, I do it. Kyle's course had seven instructional videos with writing activities at the end, but one video in particular stuck with me and still does today. In these videos Kyle talks about allowing the anxiety to come through. In my mind, I thought, *"Why the fuck would I **want** it to come, all I wanted was for it to go away."* Kyle describes being in a pool of water with ripples and waves all around you. Then he asks how do you get them to stop? You simply sit and allow. Allow the ripples to come around you and eventually the water will become still.

I was in my senior year of college at the time with anxiety for days so to speak. I was still accepting and trying to heal from my brother's suicide attempts and trying to focus on graduating college. I was in one of my psychology classes one day and, as anyone who has dealt with anxiety knows, panic attacks can creep up out of nowhere. I felt a tingling in my toes shoot up my legs into the pit of my stomach and up to my chest where it began to tighten and my heart started to race. My eyes darted around to see if there was anything dangerous, and of course, there wasn't. I thought of Kyle. His voice came into my head about the ripples in the water and sitting still and most importantly allowing. So, I was sitting in class clearly not paying attention to the lecture, but I sat and allowed. I was breathing deeply and slowly; I surrendered to the anxiety and allowed it to come. It was the first time in years that my anxiety immediately went away. I didn't have to take Xanax, which usually gave me an immediate fix. I was able to *control* my anxiety in a different, healthier way. I was elated, and I practiced Kyle's technique every day or any time I felt anxious. Of course, I realized that nothing is overnight, and I knew I had to practice these skills in order to manage my anxious thoughts and symptoms.

I looked up some of Kyle's videos on YouTube to see more of what he was about. I saw one video of him doing a speech at some conference, and I immediately loved what he was saying. I don't even think I finished watching the whole thing, but I remember I got an anxious feeling in my chest. But not the kind of anxiety I was used to getting… it was my intuition coming back to guide me. I looked on Kyle's website and bought a ticket to his event. I was flying to L.A. by myself to a weekend seminar called Escape from Mediocrity with hundreds of people I had never met.

I felt anxious the whole flight not knowing what I was getting myself into. I couldn't wait to get off the plane and check into my room to relax. I was nervous about being at this event by myself, and having to interact with people I didn't know. I told myself, *you traveled and backpacked to another country. You didn't have a problem meeting people then. Think of it like your travels.* I flew in the day before the event because Kyle was hosting a reception party before the event started. It was outside in the pool area with comfy couches and private cabanas. I felt awkward being there as I observed everyone seemed to have brought someone with them. I sat nearby getting warm by the firepit until a guy approached me. He would later become one of the biggest love experts, 'Create the Love.' He asked, "Why are you sitting all alone?"

I just smiled and said, "I don't know." He seemed nice and said, "Come on over and I'll introduce you to some people." I felt like I had reverted back to my shy high school self, whom I thought I had grown from. He introduced me to this woman, who's a comedian in the San Francisco area, Sandy Stec. She was silly and sarcastic and I said, "You remind me of Jersey. I love your sense of humor."

She clenched her chest, "Oh my God, that's such a compliment, thank you!" I laughed out loud and fell in love with her vibe instantly. She said, "Let's go to the lobby bar and grab a drink." She mentioned she came alone too and I knew we would be newfound besties for the weekend. I took a deep breath in relief that I had someone to hang out with.

There was another guy at the bar who was loud joking with everyone around him. He came over to Sandy and I to introduce himself. "Hi, I'm Damien." He looked like a surfer with his messy blonde-ish hair. He was even wearing no shoes.

Sandy immediately whispered to my ear, "I think he likes you."

I said, "Cut it out, he's just being friendly." Kyle then walked up to the bar. He's a celebrity to me and I felt weird about talking to him. But I wanted to tell him how happy I was that I had made it out to his event. He noticed me sitting with Sandy and he started walking over to me. He said hello to everyone who was around us and said, "Are you Laura Vaisman?" I was caught by surprise that he knew my name. He said, "You were the very first person to buy a ticket to my event." I told him I was so compelled after watching his videos and finishing the program he gave to me that I bought a ticket the next second. Kyle said, "I'm so happy you came all the way out here alone," and gave me the biggest hug. His energy was so warm, comforting, and positive that I felt better about making the decision to come out here.

The seminar was about learning how to stay in the moment, let go of fear, and follow your gut. I got to hear legends speak, such as Kelly Carlin (daughter of legendary comedian, George Carlin), Glenn Moreshower, Dick Gregory, and many more. They all have been through so much in their lives, careers, relationships, and yet they did not allow fear or struggle stop them from achieving their dreams. They taught me how we become so conditioned to ask people for advice and permission for something we already want to do.

"Do you think I should go?"

"If this were you, what would you do?"

Why do we ask those questions? We already know the answer. I was always taught to go with my "gut" feeling on everything. And most of the time I do, but

who doesn't have that little stupid voice inside your
head telling you:

"Are you sure you want to do this?"
"Is that really the right choice?"
"Maybe it's not a good idea."
"Don't do it."

And sadly, the annoying voice usually wins because it becomes
a vicious, never-ending cycle. Then comes the people who live
their lives with regret after the fact and wish they had made
those "gut" decisions. We can have the life we want and we
should not be afraid to leap. I get we all have responsibilities to
some degree and we can't just drop everything but we can
make those small leaps to get closer to the life we want to live.
You can still have your 'normal' nine to five while busting your
ass after hours to work on your side projects, dreams or
whatever it may be. When I went to Kyle's event on a whim, I
didn't expect to meet so many great people who were on a
similar path to me. I was scared shitless because I didn't know
anyone but I walked away from that event with a new family of
friends.

Damien and I had a spiritual connection, something I didn't expect nor was I looking for. The weekend was filled with bursting energy that could bring you to tears. I've never been in a room with so many people who wanted to help each other achieve their dreams.

On the last day, Damien and I spent most of the day together during the event. I had a few extra days in L.A. because I was going to meet my sister on her work trip but her trip was cancelled. Damien had to leave early and whispered, "I have to go. I gotta head back to San Diego."

I was still watching some of the last of the speakers on stage. I looked at him and smiled, "Oh, don't go just yet."

He said, "I'm sorry, I have my dog at home and I need to get back. Here's my number and we'll be in touch." I took it and thought back to Dominik and Matteo who had said the same thing.

The next day, Damien called me and asked if I was still in California. "Yeah, I am. I have a few days left here before I head back to NJ." He asked me if I was interested in coming to Mexico with him and his friends for a week. His friends have a beautiful villa in Cabo San Lucas. My immediate thoughts were, *I don't know this guy from a hole in the wall and he wants me to come to Mexico?* But something was telling me to do it and, then I remembered the old adventurous traveler part of me that I seemed to have lost. With the words, *Leap and the world will throw you a net* echoed in my head. I told Damien, "Let me think about it and get back to you."

After a day of thinking and being scared shitless to buy a ticket, I decided to do it. I flew back to NJ to get proper Mexico weather clothes and headed out to Cabo. I had a few connections on the way and I remember sitting in Charlotte, North Carolina, my last connection before arriving in Mexico, and I started to panic. My brother's first attempt, and the multiple ones he had years after that, caused me to overanalyze every single fucking thing because a part of me was always waiting for the other shoe to drop. I overidentified with any negative emotion I had in fear that I'd be suicidal like my brother, somehow would I be next or will something bad happen? It fucked me up for years. I called my mom crying, "I can't do this, I'm scared."

She said, "What's the worst that can happen? You have a good time? And if it's really bad just call one of us and we'll figure a way to get you back home."

She was right. I pulled myself together, took a deep breath, and boarded the plane. When I arrived in Mexico, I was concerned about how we would find each other because our phones didn't work and my flight arrived a different time than his. But the universe always finds a way. I saw him in the distance and under my breath said, *"Oh my god, thank god, he's here."* Our baggage claim terminals were right next to each other. He had a car ready for us to drive back to the villa where we would later meet up with his friends.

Mexico was hot. The weather was a scorching ninety-seven degrees every single day but not a drop of humidity. Coming from NJ with disgusting humidity, where you feel like you can't breathe, this was actually refreshing. His friends were a couple from California. She did yoga and he was an entrepreneur, whose name was Damien, too. Both Damiens loved to surf and took advantage of the huge waves while us girls sat at the pool with strong cocktails in hand. After a few hours of surfing and lounging around, we all worked up an appetite. We went back up to the villa, which was beautiful and overlooked the ocean, to freshen up before dinner. Our restaurant was located on the beach. We were surrounded by the starry night sky, the waves crashing in the background, our toes in the sand underneath our table. My attraction for Damien began to grow.

Maybe I got swept up by the ambiance and the beautiful country we were in and how good I felt taking a leap of faith to travel to another country by myself with people who I had just met. I knew with just a little bit of faith and some guts the world unfolds for you. I remembered how much I loved unknown adventures and I slowly began to feel like myself again.

Damien and I couldn't help but wonder what was going to happen after Mexico. He kept mentioning that he had a cabin in Oregon and had been wanting to go back there to fix it up for the springtime. Living in a cabin in the woods had always been a dream of mine and I was growing fond of Damien, which was an added bonus. He showed me pictures of the area. It was a beautiful wooded region with mountains in the background. Seeing the mountains reminded me of Switzerland. I felt like I was on a roll with taking leaps and thought, *Eh, what the hell, I'll give it a go*. When we parted ways from Mexico, we Skyped almost every day. I didn't know what this "*relationship*" was but I said, "I find it strange if we aren't boyfriend/girlfriend and I'm moving across the country to live

with you." A few days later, he asked me to be his girlfriend.
asked him, "Are you sure you can handle the traveler side of
me?" I had just graduated from college and wanted to live a
nomadic lifestyle.

***

He said he accepted it. At this time, I was in the
middle of getting my Italian citizenship. My sister and I
researched a loophole which would grant us citizenship via my
great grandfather. He never became a U.S. Citizen when he
came to America, which allowed his Italian citizenship to be
passed down to us. I had about six months or so left and my
plan was to move to Switzerland (more on that in Chapter 6). I
told Damien of my plans and he said to come and live with
him for the winter and then head to Switzerland in the Spring
because he wanted to stay and fix up his cabin.

The original plan was for me to drive out by myself
and meet him there. He surprised me and flew out to NJ,
which I knew was hard for him. Flying is one of his biggest
fears. It meant a lot to me that he came out. I drove to the
airport to pick him up and when I found him at the pickup
area, I got out of the car excited that he was here. When I went

to hug him, he reeked of alcohol. I said, "Are you drunk?" He lost his balance a little bit and put his bags into my car.

He said, "Yeah, and I took Xanax, too. You know how I am with flying." I understood his fear but I was a bit annoyed being that he was coming to my house to meet my family like that. I said, "I thought you wanted me to show you NYC since you've never been here."

"No, I don't give a shit about NYC." A part of me immediately wished I had told him to get back on the plane and go back home.

When we arrived at my house, I was nervous for him to meet my family in his current state. We went upstairs to my room to put his things down. I said, "Are you going to shower? You look like a mess." He shook his head no. My family came home and my dad said let's all sit on the deck for a small lunch. My sister and mother were there as well. I told Damien to gather himself and look semi-presentable because my family had just got back home. We walked outside and we all introduced ourselves. I was a nervous wreck and couldn't even bare to sit at the table. I couldn't believe this is how he wanted to present himself to my father. I knew my family could see right through him, which made me uncomfortable if I should do this or not.

A week prior to Damien flying out, my father had a heart attack and his first week back home from the hospital. It was an extremely emotional week, and now I would be leaving him and home to move 3,000 miles away. I felt so guilty to leave my dad. My dad said, "I'm okay, I want you to do this. I always wanted to drive cross-country so go. Don't stop because of me." I don't think I've ever cried so much in a week. I said my goodbyes and hugged my little puppy one last time before I left. We had to quickly get on the road in order to get to Oregon on time. Once we got on the road, things started to get real and it set in that I was really doing this. *I'm moving cross-country to live in a cabin with a guy I met for a weekend and spent a weekend in Mexico together, who happens to be fifteen years older than me.*

My family was supportive about my decision to move out west. They assured me if things didn't work out I could always come back home. I felt more at ease knowing I had my family's support no matter which way all of this went. Damien and I drove through the most beautiful parts of the country. I grew up in the suburbs in a congested area. I always yearned for nature, which was why I loved sitting in Central Park having lunch or reading a book. When I was younger, I always thought, *I want to do a road trip across country one day.*

Now I was witnessing the vast beauty of this country, something everyone needs to see. I always heard about small town America in books, school, and the media. It's a huge topic when it comes to the elections in the States. Living on the East Coast my whole life, I became accustomed to the big city life. I never understood what small towns were like or what their appeal was. Traveling across the U.S., I never realized how much of this country is run by small towns. We have big cities here and there, but in between it all are small towns. I remember driving through a town in Emblem, Wyoming, that only had a population of ten people! Experiencing small town America and taking it all in, made me appreciate them. Seeing it for myself put things into perspective and I wished my dad could see this.

The drive took us five days, which is quite fast, but Damien had his dog in Oregon, and we had to get there in time before the pet sitter left. There was a lot more of the country I wanted to see. For example, the itinerary I originally had was to go more north because I wanted to see Glacier

National Park in Montana, but Damien overtook mine with things he wanted to do. At least Mt. Rushmore was still on the list. We arrived in South Dakota and we stopped to look at Mt. Rushmore, and I wondered where it was. Some travelers walked past us and said, "You can't see it, it's too foggy." I was so upset. I secretly wanted to stay another day just to see it but Damien said we had to get back on the road.

Another interesting place we stopped was The Field of Dreams in Iowa, the *real* one. Seeing The Field of Dreams was an emotional moment for Damien. The unfortunate part is we didn't know each other well enough, but I knew it meant a lot to him and brought up memories of his childhood with his father. We were in the hotel and I grabbed my bag to pack the car and I turned around and he was in the fetal position on the bed in tears. I thought, *"Whaaat the fucckk?"* I was more confused then anything because a moment ago he was fine. I tried to console him and asked him what was wrong. He didn't want to tell me what it was. But I could only assume it was because of the anticipation of seeing the field and it was his childhood dream to go there.

When we got there, I could see his eyes light up in awe, like a child seeing Disneyland for the first time. The field is exactly what it was in the movie. We took off our shoes and ran through the grass to the corn fields where Damien ran into and then ran back out like in the movie. We had baseball gloves and played catch in the outfield. The sun was shining, other families were there playing with their kids and running the bases.

Damien was great with people, especially kids. He was like a big kid himself, and he saw one dad in particular not paying attention to his son when his son asked to play catch. Damien went up to the kid and asked if he wanted to run around the bases with him and play catch. The kid's smile went from side to side with excitement. I was at home plate watching them run around the bases and when the boy came to third base, his face was filled with joy. I loved how Damien did random acts of kindness. I bet that little boy was so happy the rest of the day and perhaps he will never forget the moment he had at The Field of Dreams.

***

The rest of our drive was filled with listening to Pandora comedy skits, which kept us awake and laughing most of the way. After five days of driving, we finally arrived in

Brightwood, Oregon. The sun was shining, the air was fresh with the river flowing in the distance. I thought, *Ahh, this is it. This is where I need to be.* We weren't completely isolated as I had imagined, we had neighbors but it was like a small village. We had Mount Hood in the distance, which was one of my favorite things about Brightwood. It was so small that it was about one street long. It had local stores not too far away but no stores I recognized. If I wanted to find a chain grocery store and some civilization, I had to drive thirty minutes to the next town.

I enjoyed the beautiful setting, but reality was becoming reality. Damien and I were living together after only knowing each other maybe two or three months, and not having a solid foundation was becoming an issue. Our backgrounds and life situations were just *different.* Damien was used to working from home and being an entrepreneur, whereas I moved out there with no job and about $6,000 in my account I was saving for Switzerland. I tried looking for anything out there, but I honestly didn't know what jobs to look for. I always loved doing photography, preferably film photography. Damien wanted to help me become my own boss and start something with my photography, but I wasn't about it. I liked doing photography as a hobby and I was okay with not getting paid for it. I called my dad one day and asked what I should do. My dad said he knew someone who worked at the FBI office in Portland. Damien was not fond of the idea of me working at the FBI office.

***

After I got off the phone with my dad, I went to Damien to tell him of some good news. "I think I may have a hook up at the FBI office in Portland, I have my B.A. degree in Forensic Psychology, so maybe I could work there." Damien was quiet for a moment and paced the living room and said, "No girlfriend of mine is working for the FBI." I was beginning to see a side of Damien I didn't like. I didn't know what he expected I'd do there, just stay home and be a housewife?

I was twenty-three years old, independent with a huge free spirit. I started to see our age gap was becoming an issue, too. We were on different pages in our lives – more like chapters, even. He wanted to settle down and have a family. I, on the other hand, didn't want kids or to settle down. I was annoyed because I told him all of this when we were in Mexico and he said he was cool with it.

Eleven or so days after arriving there, I did not want to be there. I was a morning person and loved to work out when I got up, whereas he liked to sleep in and work on his laptop in bed, sometimes even when I was still sleeping. He smoked an ungodly amount of weed, which made him lazy in my opinion. Damien overtook the upstairs part of the cabin and made the room into his "man cave/office." I didn't feel included in anything. I felt like I was just staying there on an extended stay, not "*living together.*" The "spiritual" Damien I met back in L.A. was not here.

There is always a risk you take when you don't know someone well. Our fights were filled with anger and misunderstandings. I didn't feel comfortable being with someone who became so angry over little things. Damien is not a bad person, we just moved too fast and didn't have the foundation to make our relationship work. We had a fight one particular night where we were yelling and screaming. He stomped his way upstairs and slammed the door. I let him have some time to cool off and came to find him sleeping. I said, "What the hell was that? I think we should talk calmly to each other." He was upset that I wanted to leave and go to Switzerland at some point.

I said, "But you knew that! I told you." He grew angry. He sat up and clenched his fists. For some reason, my mind began registering what was going on and everything slowed down around me as I was preparing myself for him to hit me or something. Thankfully, he didn't. He stormed out of the house hours after that and I didn't know where he was or what he was doing. A voice came into my head and said, *"He has a gun."*

I thought back to a conversation we had over Skype when I was still living in NJ where he was joking around mentioning he was going to bring his gun to the cabin. I'm sure my studies from school have something to do with it, but I never felt comfortable with the idea of having a gun in the home. I began looking everywhere in the house where he could possibly hide it. I started in his office, I went through little attic crawl spaces. I opened a small closet, got a chair and stood on it to see what was on the top shelf. *There it was.* A typical handgun similar to what police officers use along with a box of bullets and a lot of them. The gun was not locked in a proper lockbox and it may or may not have been fully loaded, but the safety was not on. I grew anxious and uncomfortable.

I did not tell him why I was leaving, I just packed my things and went to California where my brother lived. A year prior my brother decided he needed to get away from NJ and all the negativity. He enrolled in culinary school and found a job as a chef in a restaurant. Everyone said I was doing the right thing. And it did feel right. I was scared and didn't feel safe so I left. But even as I was leaving I felt so much goodness.

I had a ten hour drive ahead of me, and I kid you not, I saw rainbows, even double rainbows, the *entire* way to my brother's place. I started crying in my car because I knew I was making the right choice and I was being guided somewhere. I stopped in Redding, California after driving seven hours straight to catch some rest at a hotel near the highway. I was disappointed and shocked that I had no messages from Damien, not even a call or text to see where I was or to see if I was okay.

By the next afternoon, I arrived at my brother's place, not welcomed at first. When I later found out he had a bad day at work and I showed up at the wrong time, it made me feel even worse. I felt like I had nowhere to go. *Great, even my own brother doesn't want me here.* It was a scary moment and I began researching for trucks to pick up my car and ship it back to NJ.

But then I started hanging out with my brother's friends from his church. I'm not religious at all, but I thought to myself, just be open you may hear messages you need to hear. His friends, Nick and James were great people. We all did a hike together at Mission Peak. We woke up at 4:30 a.m. and met at the mountain at 5:00 a.m. to try to make it to the top in time to see the sun rise. It was not a small hike. As James said, it was rough but not that bad. I needed something physical after feeling so emotional the last few days.

We finally made it to the top and waited for the sun to rise. Out of nowhere, the clouds were moving over us so fast, we were engulfed in them. It was like waves of clouds crashing over our heads. I have never seen anything like that in my life. They said it was God, but it didn't matter to me what they called it, we all felt something. We all felt connected together. A man up was up there with us said, "I've climbed this mountain forty times and I've never witnessed this." It gave me the emotional strength and validation that everything was going to be ok. The next day my brother took me to his church. It was the first time I stepped in a church since I was five years old. I went in there with an open mind, wanting to see what my brother was enjoying. The pastor spoke about enjoying the journey, life is an adventure. Just relax. And God gives us "Divine Delays," something is delayed because something else needs to happen first. And I truly believe me leaving Damien and coming to my brother was so I could be there to hear that.

***

I went to a Bible study group one night with my brother. Steven knows I'm not into the whole church thing, but I thought I'd go and see what it was all about. The people were so welcoming and warm, and even though I didn't see eye to eye on their beliefs, we had one thing in common... to love people, even people who are strangers to you. I felt comfortable with them, and I can see why my brother was drawn to them.

A woman was sitting next to me and said, "My daughter brought me to this, it's very nice to meet Steven's sister, he spoke highly of you. What brought you here?" I told her I just left my boyfriend and drove all the way down here alone not knowing what or where to go. She said, "Have faith and trust." Her comforting words eased my worries. When we left the Bible study, she slipped $40.00 into my hand. I said, "Oh, no, I can't accept this. I really appreciate it." She insisted. I eventually took it and gave her a big hug.

She said, "You know what decision you have to make; it's all completely up to you."

After spending time with these wonderful people, I started wondering if I had made a mistake. I spoke with Damien and I's mutual friend, Kyle (from the Escape from Mediocrity weekend) who put things into perspective for me coming from a guy. He assured me he knew Damien for a long time and he would never hurt me. I wanted to make things work and did not want to leave to go home without having given it a proper shot. Both of us storming out of the house didn't solve anything. I decided to go back. My gut told me to. I had plenty of people telling me otherwise, that I deserved and could do so much better. Maybe they were right, maybe they weren't, but it would bother me if I didn't try. I said my goodbyes to my brother and his friends who were so good to me and took me in as a friend and showed me how to have faith, to forgive and trust in the process of life. I packed up my car again and headed out for another ten to eleven hour drive back to Brightwood. Driving back felt good and being in his arms after a spiritual couple of days felt reassuring. We started doing things as a couple. You would think doing things together would have been a given, but it just wasn't before. Life was good, at least for a little while.

***

Then sometimes life throws you another curveball straight to the face and sometimes you just have to listen to what it's telling you. After bringing up my plans to travel the world and go to Switzerland, it brought up another argument of why I had come back. I wanted to talk about my travel plans with Damien, I wanted him to get excited about traveling, about *us* traveling together. He didn't. I had a hard time understanding his lack of enthusiasm because I told him from day one I'm a traveler and if he didn't like that part of me then don't get into a relationship with me. But he did. I felt played in a way. I thought, *why did you have me leave my family to move across the country to live with you if you didn't like a big part of who I am?* He said, "I don't want to be with someone who doesn't want to be here or is planning to leave." I guess we both misunderstood the plan of us going to Oregon. I told him Switzerland was always a part of my plan. I didn't say it but in my mind I knew Switzerland had to be a solo trip, which made it wrong of me to go out to Oregon with him. However, Damien told me to stay for the winter and then go to Switzerland. We never really discussed anything further, and I think we both knew this wasn't going to work for good this time.

I started going on hikes by myself. Brightwood was walking distance to a national park, so I'd work out in the mornings and go out for a hike into nature. Nature is where I can connect with my soul and earth's energy. I go there to clear my head from the madness and receive guidance. I called my cousin back home and felt I was seeking validation and permission to leave. My gut knew the answer, but I was scared to do it. I felt stupid for coming out there and going back to him. I could have stayed in San Jose with my brother and tried to make things work out there or, better yet, I should have gone on my own road trip back home. I was beginning to realize after years of losing myself, intuition always knows the answer, but before I never listened, hence the anxiety and fear.

I was taking chances, taking risks on love (whether they were good decisions or not). But one thing I've learned on my journey is that you can't play the "What If" game. You'll never win. We have to learn to accept things as they are. Worrying about what could have been will only drive you crazy. Whether it's good or bad, accepting as is a lot easier in the long run than wondering, "What if?"

I cannot think of this as bad thing even though I may feel disappointed about it. It truly was and is a blessing in disguise. I believe everything happens for a reason and we don't meet people by accident. Everyone you meet serves a purpose in your life, whether it's meant to be for a lifetime or few a months, days, weeks, minutes or seconds. Everyone plays a part of giving you a lesson, but it's *you* who has to be aware of it happening and open to seeing it. Damien is a beautiful person, and all I could wish for him is happiness one day with a woman who suits his needs and wants in a relationship, and I know he would wish the same for me. It's unfortunate when you have a different picture in your head of how things will be and they become the complete opposite. I did not expect us to part so soon, but we did, and I accepted it.

I can only be grateful for the beautiful experiences, both the good and the ugly, because it showed me how to better myself.

Chapter 6: How I Became an Italian Citizen

2013

"If you don't recount your family history, it will be lost. Honor your own stories and tell them too. The tales may not seem very important, but they are what binds families and makes each of us who we are." -Madeleine L'Engle

My great grandfather, Alessandro, was born in Palermo, Sicily. I always wondered about the history of my Italian side. I had a deep love for Europe and wanted to live there one day ever since I was little. I always had a feeling that there had to be a way or some kind of loophole where my family could become Italian citizens. I was still attending college at the time and saving any money I could. I received a phone call one day from my lawyer about a car accident I had on Thanksgiving day back in 2010. I had won my case. I T-boned someone after they ran a light and totaled my car, suffering whiplash, a small concussion and a bulging disc in my spine. My lawyer informed me I had received ten thousand dollars for the damages. I couldn't believe it.

My case was open for two years and a few days prior I had thought about giving him a call to close my case. After the lawyer fees, I was left with six thousand dollars. I put the money right into my savings account and didn't touch it except to add any money I had for Europe.

My sister, Eva and I, began our family research in 2008 after I came home from my backpacking trip throughout Europe. I remembered the promise I made to the boss, Luca, at The Funny Farm to come back to work there with my European passport.

An Italian guy named Marco, who lived in Naples, added me randomly on Facebook one day. Marco desperately wanted to come to the U.S. to live, work, and go to school at USC. Little did I know how Marco and I met was not so random. He wanted me to help him edit his admissions letter for the school since his English wasn't good at the time. We became good friends, joked about us getting married to swap citizenships, and exchanged stories about life in America and Italy.

After speaking to family members, all we knew was my great grandfather was born in Palermo. We knew his birth date, but weren't quite sure of the year. It was either 1893 or 1895.

Marco called the consulate in Palermo to find out more information about what to do. He contacted me back and said I had to write a letter explaining what I'm looking for with names and dates along with three international coupons.

Trying to find international coupons was like trying to find a needle in a haystack, mainly because no one knew what they were. I called many local post offices and finally found one twenty minutes away from where I lived in NJ. The international coupons were like postage stamps for Italy to send back documents. Marco said he would write the letter for me in Italian. I gave him all the information I had on my great grandfather, and then the only thing I could do was hope we got something in the mail.

Eva and I were taking a risk; we felt like we were holding our breath for the next two weeks. I constantly checked the mailbox for anything from Italy and then one day we got something. As I opened the envelope from Comune di Palermo, my heart was beating with excitement. I pulled out a letter I couldn't understand, but alongside it was an *original* copy. I couldn't believe it!

I helped Marco with his admissions letter to USC, and he responded to me a few days later letting me know that he was accepted. I was so happy for him. His dream of going to USC and coming to America were coming true as were mine of becoming a European citizen. I believe Marco and I were brought together for a reason. Maybe it was the spirit of my great grandfather who helped us help each other achieve our dreams. The amount of gratitude I have for Marco cannot be put into words; if it wasn't for him, I wouldn't have been able to get this process started. Eva and I were researching for days, weeks, months, and years to figure out the process of getting our Italian citizenship. I found the consulate website to double check we were eligible and found there were five different categories.

We fell under category five, which stated, "Your direct paternal or maternal ancestors were born in the United States from Italian parents. They never renounced their right to Italian citizenship." I had to make sure when my great grandfather came to this country he never became naturalized. I researched where you can find naturalization papers because my great grandfather originally came to New York City. I found The National Archives where the woman at the front desk did the search in New York City and Washington D.C. to make sure there were no documents stating he became a naturalized citizen.

A few weeks later, we received a letter saying they could not find a record of him, which was great news and I told the woman prior to leaving I needed a letter stating she did the search and didn't find anything. Now we were officially able to continue our search. Tracing each step of him coming to America was quite an experience. I unfortunately never got to meet my great grandfather, but I know he would be proud of the hard work we did to become Italian citizens. Every document had to link back to Alessandro, each document was the next puzzle piece, a timeline if you will, of him all the way down to us.

To start, we had to get my grandfather's birth and death certificate. My grandfather lived in Carteret, NJ, and we figured we get his documents from there. When we went to the consulate in Newark, NJ, they didn't accept it because the documents had to be from the State of NJ, not a local town. We went to the vital statistics office in Trenton and filled out the application to request my grandfather's birth and death certificate. Each document took two weeks to get and then we needed to get them officially sealed with an apostille seal in a different office in Trenton, which took another two weeks. Also, each document in English needed to be translated into Italian to be sent back to Italy to be approved. The consulate gave us an Italian woman named Annemarie, who was huge part of our application process. She lived in Paramus, NJ, about forty to fifty minutes from where I lived. We had to drive back and forth to Trenton and Paramus for our documents.

Overall, we had to get other documents for my grandfather and his marriage, my mother's birth certificate, her marriages and divorces along with Eva's birth certificate, mine and Steven's. We made copies of every document we ordered.

Eva and I were becoming regulars at the Italian consulate in Newark. We walked into the door up to a glass window with four little tiny holes to speak into. They would walk past the door, glance at us, and continue to walk away. There were times where I had to yell through the tiny holes to get someone's attention when we had an appointment and would sit there for over an hour before anyone took notice that we were sitting there. Rita, an employee handling our case at the consulate, was extremely rude and acted like we were no better than a piece of gum on her shoe. We wanted to ask what was happening with our documents since we sent everything in, and we were told they were mailed to Italy. Rita told us with her heavy Italian accent, "You're missing documents." I knew, for a fact, it wasn't true since I made copies of everything I gave to her. She was lying and either threw them out or misplaced them on purpose. Rita made it difficult for us to get our citizenship, but it only made me more determined to be persistent.

Rita was my test of how bad I wanted this citizenship, how bad I wanted to go to Europe and live there. I refused to let her ruin my chance of being an Italian citizen. We had to get the document again through Trenton to request the document, get the apostille seal, get it translated, and send it back to Rita. We did whatever it took.

If our journey to becoming Italian citizens couldn't have been any more frustrating, all of a sudden, the consulate in Newark shut down. It felt like a stab in the heart. I thought, *How are we going to get this now?* After calling them relentlessly and hearing no response, I went down to the consulate myself only to find a paper on the door saying all of our documents were moved to the NYC consulate. Newark was only twenty minutes or so from where I lived, so it wasn't as difficult to commute back and forth, but now we'd have to take the train an hour to the consulate in the city. I feared they had lost our documents. We were finally at the end, we had heard from Italy and everything was approved; all we needed was our passports.

On March 13th, 2014, was my appointment with the NYC Italian consulate. I considered taking the train, but I didn't want to risk any delays, so I drove in, making sure to get up extra early so I wouldn't be late. I found parking right next to the consulate, not caring how much it would be, and I went inside. I had all my documents with me, copies and all. The room was packed with people, and I found a seat next to this little Italian woman. I was a ball of nerves waiting for my name to be called.

"VAISMAN! Someone who worked at the consulate yelled across the room. My heart began to race, and I grabbed all my documents. I sat down with a man who barely asked me any questions, which was strange because the people at Newark acted like the CIA. He asked for my identification, my birth certificate, and passport. Everything around me slowed down, and all I could concentrate on was his hand stamping my documents, which read, "APPROVED." Tears were beginning to well up as he approved my application. I composed myself enough to hand him over my money. "One hundred and eight U.S. dollars, please," he said. He handed me a receipt, and told me I would be contacted when it was ready. I called my mom first in the happiest of tears. I was finally approved, but I couldn't celebrate just yet, not until I had it physically in my hands.

I was obsessively checking the mailbox for anything from the Italian consulate, and to my surprise only four days later I received something in the mail. I ripped the package as if I were opening a Willy Wonka bar looking for the golden ticket. I saw a red passport peek through, and I cried. All the hard work was worth it. My dream had come true, and I could finally proudly say I was an Italian citizen. Five years is a long time, but when you want something bad enough you will do whatever it takes to make it happen. I was finally going back to Switzerland as an Italian citizen to work at The Funny Farm like I said six years ago.

All of this proved to me we can achieve the dreams we have. Yes, it requires work, patience and maybe some tears and dark times where you want to give up, but persistence is what gets you there. I never gave up on wanting to live and work in

Switzerland. I thought about it every day for those six years, and now I would be going back. This time, it was my first solo backpacking trip.

Chapter 7: A Bittersweet Goodbye

2014

"Don't be afraid of change, because it is leading you to a new beginning."-
Joyce Meyer

I had been friends with a famous Swiss singer for quite
a few years. We would chat here and there about life in the
U.S. and Switzerland. We'd have deep conversations about
life's philosophical questions about life and death, heaven and
hell, and what we believe happens to us after we leave this
beautiful planet. At times, I'd help him fix his songs he wrote
in English to flow better grammatically and lyrically. Levin was
a sweet, shy guy; his talent overshadowed his awkwardness. His
guitar and pen in hand, his confidence and true self illuminated
the room.

After becoming friends via Facebook, we finally met
in person. When I had my official date to fly to Switzerland, I
immediately messaged him. He was so happy for me. April 7th,
2014, I packed one bag with no plan, no job, and no place to

live with only the faith that everything would work out when I got there. Six years of waiting and I'd finally be back in Interlaken but this time as an Italian citizen. After I told Levin the news, he offered to host me. I wasn't expecting him to offer nor was I planning on asking him. I had hostels lined up, but I gratefully accepted his offer, plus it would be nice for us to finally meet. "Great, I will pick you up from the airport in Zurich… just send me your flight info so I can keep track of when you land." I sent him my flight information and tried to get some sleep for my flight.

I barely slept. I woke up, packed my bag into the car, and my dad drove with me to the airport. I was beyond excited. I asked my dad, "Are you ok with me doing this?"

He said, "Yeah, I just want you to be safe, that's all. Just stay in touch." When we arrived at JFK airport, my dad walked me in before the security checkpoints. My nerves kicked into high gear. I started to cry as I was waiting in line.

"I'm scared," I told my dad. He was surprised by my change in emotions. I was holding it in while we were driving in the car. I was sad to leave my dad and I was scared if this didn't work out. My dad hugged me and said, "Don't worry, you'll be fine. This is what you wanted. Everything will work out. I love you. Now go have a good time."

I knocked out on the flight and woke up in Switzerland. I remembered Zurich airport from my People to People trip and was flooded with memories. I had a phone with me this time but I didn't have a sim card. I stopped at the sim card window to buy one so I could have a Swiss number and get in touch with Levin. I didn't see him anywhere so I walked outside towards the parking garage. I recognized him from pictures on Facebook and yelled out, "Levin?" He turned around, smiled, and walked over to me.

He gave me a big hug and said, "It's so nice to finally meet you in person." He grabbed my bags and asked, "Are you hungry?" After fifteen hours of flying, I'd say I was more than hungry… I was starving. He drove me to downtown Zurich and I didn't remember this at all when I was here a few years ago. It just like any other main city, lots of restaurants and bars. He took me to a small Italian restaurant where I had a big bowl of pasta with sauce and fresh kiwi juice. It was the best kiwi juice I've ever had.

All of my senses were heightened. I felt like I could breathe better because of the crisp mountain air. Everything seemed to taste better because it was foreign to me, and my heart was light and filled with excitement to be back and make this place my home. We didn't stay too long at dinner. Levin could sense I was growing tired and suggested heading home. Levin's home was gorgeous. Modern, with big glass windows and stone walls overlooking the lake. I thought to myself, *Not bad for not having a plan.* Levin knew I was heading to Interlaken and he said, "If you like, I'm heading towards Interlaken and I could drop you off." He already offered to pick me up from the airport and let me stay in his home. I said, "Oh, that's so nice of you. But you've done a lot for me already. Don't worry, I'll take the train." He insisted. I obliged and said, "Well at the very least let me pay for gas."

Before we went to bed, he offered to make me some tea and set me up downstairs to sleep where he has small concerts in his home, he asked if I could help him with his lyrics. Jetlag was setting in but I felt I owed him after all he'd done for me so far. I was flattered he wanted my help. I said, "Of course." I waited for him to set up his guitar. He strung the strings and played a silly tune to hear the notes and began singing some of his songs. His voice was beautiful and everything musical seemed so effortless for him. I closed my eyes and focused on the melody and the lyrics to see if any of the words needed to be changed. Small grammatical errors, sentence structure, some words and phrases were difficult to translate from Swiss German to English. I would watch his hands move along the strings in a meticulous way as he produced angelic music. Levin was a different person when he played his guitar, his passion surrounding him and anyone listening. "Merci, thank you, for helping me with my lyrics."

I said, "No need to thank me, you're letting me stay in your home, it's nothing. We smiled at each other and I fell into a deep, jet lag-induced slumber.

Prior to leaving the states, Matteo reached out to me. He saw on Facebook that I was in Zurich. He said, "You're more than welcome to stay with me for a little while when you get to Interlaken until you find a flat (apartment) and work." I was a little surprised to hear from him being that we hadn't talked much since our drunken fight six years ago. I had a lot of emotions come up. I wasn't eighteen anymore, but parts of me still had feelings for him. I felt like there was unfinished business between us. I didn't know if Matteo and I were just some summer fling or something more, and to be honest I wasn't sure if he still felt the same way after all this time. I was curious and said, "Wow, well it's great to hear from you. It'd be nice to catch up. Thank you."

Levin drove me to Interlaken Ost train station. I said, "Thank you so much for driving me. Please take some gas money."

He smiled and shook his head, "No worries, maybe we'll see each other in a different part of the world. You can buy me a beer and we can call it even." I gave him a big hug and thanked him again for the drive and letting me stay with him.

***

Matteo texted me back saying he'd be at the train station to pick me up shortly. I was excited and apprehensive. I told myself, *just have no expectations*. I saw him drive around the bend looking for me, he lowered his head to see where I was standing, we caught each other's eye and smiled at each other. He circled back around and stopped where I stood. He got out of the car, walked around, and gave me a hug. He looked the same, just a little older and subdued. He seemed genuinely happy to see me and asked, "Do you mind coming to the grocery store with me? I'll cook us lunch." I shook my head in agreement.

We didn't talk much in the car. To break the awkward silence I said, "You look good, Matteo. It's good to see you again."

He looked over at me, smiled and said, "Yeah, you too." We walked into the store and he went off looking for things to cook. I was behind him looking all the different Swiss foods. "Do you know what you'd like?"

"No, I'm not too picky. We could just barbeque and roast some veggies. I'll get wine." The normalcy we both were playing was driving me crazy. My mind was racing with curiosity, *What is he thinking?* I couldn't read him.

When we got back to the car, Matteo said, "My girlfriend is out of town for work but she'll be back in a few days. She knows you're staying here and she can't wait to meet you. You'll like her." My heart sank. I was silent for a few seconds trying to withhold my disappointment.

"Ohh, that's cool. How long have you guys been together?"

He said, "Five years." I thought, "*Well, fuck. There goes any kind of chance of rekindling anything.*" We were quiet for the remainder of the short car drive to his home. Again, almost anyone's home is gorgeous in Switzerland because the scenery is unbelievable; Swiss Alps everywhere.

We set up the barbeque outside in his garden, I grabbed the wine. "Can I open this?" He ran inside to grab the bottle opener and the rest of the grilling tools. I needed a glass of wine to settle my nerves. I watched him cook as I prepared and chopped the veggies. We let the meats and veggies cook and took a seat on the table. Matteo lit a spliff looking out into the distance pacing back and forth a little bit and then came sat down across from me. I could sense he was a little nervous too. "So, what's been going on with you these last six years?" I chuckled.

He laughed, "I know it's been a long ass time. I can't believe you're back." We gave each other an overview of what our lives had been like all these years and sat back to enjoy the moment.

A whole bottle of wine between us, we went inside because it was getting chilly. He suggested, "Hey let's watch a movie. And smoke a spliff." I was drunk enough and didn't want to smoke, but we watched a 3D movie. How we both didn't throw up was beyond me. Another bottle of wine later, we sat on his couch with our 3D glasses on covered in blankets. His arms were crossed, trying not to lean into me, but I felt his fingers through his jacket caressing my arm. I didn't think much of it, and I began stretching out my legs a little bit since he decided to watch a two hour movie. My foot accidentally bumped into his. I laughed, "Sorry, I need to stretch for a sec. We've been sitting too long." Matteo didn't say anything and touched my foot back. Once again, I didn't think anything of it. After the movie was over, he leaned over to me and hugged me. My heart began to race from being caught off guard. I thought, "*Shit. We shouldn't do this. I know what he's doing. Maybe he really did like me all this time. What if his girlfriend comes home early and sees us?*" But then I thought, "*Cut it out, it's just a hug.*"

Matteo said, "I like you." I giggled out of nervousness but also happy he said that.

I jokingly said, "Yeah? Still, after all this time?"

Matteo said, "Yeah."

I said, "You've always been in the back of my mind over the years.

He leaned back and came in to hug me again but this time it was a longer hug. I thought, *Shit. This is going to go a way I initially wanted, but not under these circumstances.*

***

He leaned in and kissed me. I had waited six years to kiss him again. I was conflicted, *oh this is good but no this isn't good, he has a girlfriend. Fuck, what do I do?* Matteo said, "You're more than welcome to come upstairs and watch some TV with me." I wasn't sure if I wanted to indulge, but the wine was talking, and I decided to. We wanted to have sex but wound up hooking up in other ways. We laid in bed cuddling. He was dragging his fingers over my stomach and making gentle circles around my belly button.

He said, "This was so lovely." He started telling me about his girlfriend and that they had a complicated relationship. I stayed quiet because I didn't know how much he was willing to disclose. He went on to say, "She did some fucked up shit to me in the past."

I immediately said, "Is this revenge for what she did?" He said, "No, it's not. But I don't want either of us to give our hopes up." I didn't know how to react to that. A part of me of was naive and in denial that he was just sleeping with me to sleep with me. I believed we had a connection all those years ago and perhaps me coming back would refuel that. I honestly don't know why I couldn't let the notion of us being something more go. Matteo said, "You can stay here and sleep next to me if you like." Slightly annoyed at what he said to me, I thought it wasn't a good idea and slept downstairs.

The next morning, I did my yoga routine outside in the garden. Matteo came outside with some tea and coffee. There was an awkward energy. Matteo said, "I can't act the way I did with you last night when my girlfriend comes back." I thought, *"Yeah, no shit."* I was growing increasingly annoyed with his nonchalant behavior. He said, "Let's go watch a movie." *I guess this is code for sex?* I looked at him with a suspicious glare. He laughed a little, "We won't do anything." We watched a documentary about a singer in South Africa that was famous but he didn't know it. Despite what Matteo discussed with me in the garden, he remained close to me. Of course, I wanted to be close to him but I was trying my hardest not to succumb to his advances. He ran his fingers through my hair and lightly put his finger under my chin, kissed me, and apologized.

I said, "Why are you apologizing?"

He said, "I don't know. This is dangerous." And then he kissed me a few more times. I pretended I was getting tired from the movie and told him I was going to bed. He asked, "You gonna come upstairs?"

I said, "No, I'll sleep down here."

***

In the morning, Matteo left a little early to go pick up his girlfriend. I felt pressured and a little uncomfortable staying in the house from the recent encounters Matteo and I had. When he left, I headed into town in Interlaken to look for work and get my own place. It was surreal to be back in Interlaken. I felt like I was seeing flashbacks of 2008 when I first arrived as a backpacker. I walked through the front of The Mattenhof and felt a sense of accomplishment that I had made it. I kept my word and made it back to The Funny Farm. I walked around the back to see if there was anyone I'd recognize that still worked there. I found the manager, Luca, in the garden watering the flowers. I said, "Luca?" He turned around and looked at me for a second. I said, "Do you remember me? It's Laura." He immediately gave me a big hug and invited me inside to have a beer. I saw my old friends, Johnny and Nick, whom I hadn't seen in years. We chatted and I told Luca, "So, I was able to become an EU citizen, I have my Italian passport, I'd love to work here."

Luca smiled, "I knew you'd do it. And of course you can work here. You can even stay in the back. Johnny will show you to your room." In a matter of five minutes, I found a job and a place to stay. Johnny set up my room card and asked what room I'd like. I said, "I'd like the room I had in 2008 if that's possible."

He said, "The card will open any door, so if you remember which room you had then go for it." I didn't remember the room number but I knew exactly where it was. He asked, "Do you need help with your bags?"

I said, "No, most of my stuff is still at Matteo's and I'll grab it later, but do you mind if I go back there to check it out?" Johnny smiled and signaled for me to go ahead. As I walked back to The Funny Farm, I was shocked at how much of this place had changed. It was devastating to see in person; I felt like the memories of this place were lost in time. There was another guy who lived in The Funny Farm, Aloise, who said they hadn't used the hostel for years. It's only used when The Mattenhof gets overly crowded during events. The Guinness tent, Space Camp were gone and hadn't been up in years.

I went back to Matteo's to tell him the good news and to gather my things to move into The Funny Farm. I took a taxi back to Matteo's house and when I walked in, Matteo's girlfriend was home. Matteo said, "Laura, this is Anita."

Anita was so sweet and welcomed me into their home. She said, "If there's anything you need please let me know. I'll make you breakfast tomorrow morning." I immediately felt like shit because I actually liked her.

I told them I wouldn't stay much longer, "I found a job and a flat, so I'll leave tomorrow morning but I really appreciate you both hosting me." Matteo and Anita were happy that I had found something so quickly.

Matteo said, "You'll have a great time living at The Funny Farm. I did it when I first worked there, it's a good time. And we'll probably see you around the hotel anyway." We continued to small talk for a bit longer and I let Matteo and Anita have their privacy.

I said, "I'm getting tired and have a long day tomorrow. Again, thank you for letting me stay." They smiled and said, "Goodnight, we'll see you in the morning."

I slept in later than I expected and gently woke up to the smell of fresh pancakes being made. I got up and walked into the kitchen to Anita making homemade pancakes. She said, "Do you want fruit and tea?"

I smiled and felt like I was back home. "Yes, please." She was so nice, I didn't understand why Matteo acted the way he did. After breakfast, I grabbed my things and went back to the hostel to move in. In the lobby of the Mattenhof, a jazz band was playing for a concert. It was all so lovely but I began to feel overwhelmed. I went into the phone booth and called my dad back home. I began crying, "I feel anxious, I don't know why."

My dad said, "You're just overly tired and it's been a busy few days. You just got there and it's a lot to take in. You need to rest." I wiped my tears and felt relieved after speaking with my dad.

I headed outside the hotel towards the back, walking on gravel pathways to open the door into the hostel. The stairways were still the same, the art murals on the walls were still there but the paint was chipping off, and a small hallway with wooden floors paved the way towards the rooms. I found the door where I stayed six years ago and walked inside. Normally it was a ten-bed dorm with bunk bed style beds. I felt like I was in a dream, and I even chose the same bunk I had before. All of these memories flooded into my head from me sitting in the window sill overlooking the Guinness Tent to write in my journal.

Johnny helped me bring my stuff and showed me the Bunny room, which used to have countless bunk beds. It was like a communal hangout spot. Now it was no longer a dorm, but a storage unit. My heart broke a little more each time I saw how the hostel wasn't what it used to be. Johnny said, "You can use anything you like in here, like a bedside table or a small lamp. I'm also just down the hall from you if you need anything."

"Thank you so much, Johnny, I really appreciate it." I stood in my room, took a deep breath, and almost wanted to pinch myself to make sure I wasn't dreaming. A wave of emotions came over me, and I didn't know what to feel or think.

Luca offered to have me work as a server for breakfast for the guests at The Mattenhof and then I'd bartend down in the Caverne at night. I had to be at the kitchen by 6:30 a.m. every morning. Luckily, I had serving experience but I wasn't sure how it would work with the language barrier. I also didn't have any work clothes. Luca introduced me to Ronja, the kitchen manager. She was nice but stern, and a little scary. She always talked to me in Swiss German and sometimes small English words she knew. Elena was an older woman, probably late 50s, early 60s, and she spoke decent English to get by. She'd be in charge if Ronja wasn't there. She was scarier than Ronja. Ronja introduced me to Elena and she sat at the table, smoking her cigarette and didn't even move to turn my way but said, "Hello." Ronja showed me the kitchen and where things were half in Swiss German and half-butchered English. I was going with the motions and knew I'd figure it out. She asked, "Do you have white work shirts?"

I said, "No I don't have any clothes for work."

She said, "I have some that fit you, I bring tomorrow. Size small?"

I said, "Thank you so much and yes, a small should work."

After getting shown the ropes, I went outside to sit and write. Nick saw me writing and asked, "Can I join you?" With his sing-songy German accent, he asked, "How do you feel being back here?"

I said, "It's strange."

He said, "Everyone says after the summer of 2008 everything went downhill, less people, less staff. But maybe it will be good again for you, but in a different way." I smiled. I had this thought in my head prior to coming back here, maybe too much of an expectation that eventually I'd bring this place back to what it was. I knew what it was and I knew what it could be. Nick said, "I'll let you continue writing, I'll see you around." I finished up writing and had an early night for my first day tomorrow.

I lived on a second floor and a bird would sing every single morning at 5:00 a.m. on the dot…that was my signal that I had a half hour left before my alarm went off. Luckily, I lived on the grounds so I had a two minute walk. Ronja and Elena immediately started yelling at me because I walked in at 6:30 a.m., which was my shift time. She said, "You need to be already here and working by 6:30 a.m." I shook my head in agreement. I barely saw backpackers anymore at the hotel, it was mostly group tours. The breakfast serving area would be busy but not to the point of busy I was used to when I used to banquet serve for weddings. Elena was non-stop nitpicking and yelling at me mostly in German that I was too slow. I was working fast but nothing I did was good enough. After being yelled at for four hours, I walked home and cried. Ever cry it out so good that you just fall asleep? Well, I took a long nap because later at night I was to work the bar for my first shift and it was their big Easter party.

Easter Sunday was one of their big parties to throw down in the Caverne. I've never bartended before and tonight would be my first shift. I was scared shitless. One, I'm horrible at math. Two, I haven't seen Swiss currency in so long nor did I know the language; three, they didn't have registers. Another Italian guy named Rico was the other bartender. He was loud and sweet with a smile always on his face. He was like a lot taller than me; had to be at least 6 foot. He was like a giant teddy bear. Rico said, "You alright?" I said I was fine even though I was freaking out on the inside. He started to put together a concoction of liquor in four small shot glasses. He looked over at me, "Come, let's take some shots. It'll calm your nerves. You'll be great. Now let's have a good fucking time!"

I'm a lightweight, alcohol and my horrible math are not a good combo. The night was fun the more I let go and got a hang of things; I even got a 26 Swiss Franc tip. The party didn't end until 10:00 a.m. the next morning. We closed up the bar, and cleaned up mess from the party. We went behind the hostel to the firepit to grill some sausages because we were starving and delirious. I was so tired I couldn't even wait for them to set up the grill and get it started. I told them I was going to forget the food and go to bed. I had to be up the next morning at 5:00 a.m.

After nine or ten straight days of working crazy hours of early and late-night shifts. I became sick. I had a bad cough that didn't seem to go away. Some of the guys from Alpinraft heard me coughing and asked, "Is it dry? Your cough?"

I said, "Yeah, why?"

They said, "Oh you got the Interlaken cough, they also call it the cheese cough, or the dry River cough. Everyone gets it at least once a season, but the longer you stay here you won't get it anymore." For three solid months, I had this cough that would make my ribs sore and there was nothing I could do but wait it out. I was beginning to get used to the swing of things with serving and bartending but it was starting to wear on me. Spiritually, I was struggling. I was overly tired of being overly tired, not getting enough sleep from work and my cough, being yelled at every morning for not working faster (to their standards), and criticized for every single thing I did. I was going out with old friends and meeting new ones, drinking more than I normally did at home. Most of the people I knew in Interlaken, if not everyone, loved to drink, and if I didn't accept their invite, I felt guilty like I was being impolite if I said no. I eventually grew tired of the craziness and quit.

***

I moved to The River Lodge, which was beautiful and quiet. I lived in a tiny house on a campsite, fitting only a queen-sized bed and a mini fridge. I had my own little sanctuary. The house even had a tiny porch where it fit two chairs and a small table where I could write or watch movies. I was right next to the river and it was relaxing most of the time except in the morning when the steamboats would come by blowing their horns. I was working for The River Lodge in exchange for room and board. Any odd jobs, the owner needed for me to do, I did. But, it wasn't often. And my money was slowly depleting.

I went back to The Mattenhof to see what people were up to and who was around. As I walked into the lobby, I saw Matteo was already in rare form, drunk as usual. When he was drunk though, it was like truth serum and his feelings for me always came out. But I was over his drunken antics and him going M.I.A., acting cold towards me the next day. I was seeing a similar pattern from him six years ago.

But, before I made a decision that I was probably going to leave Interlaken all together to find work somewhere else, I wanted to hang out with Matteo one last time. He came to my little house, had some wine, and we talked. Matteo drunkenly moved in to kiss me and I went with it. We began getting hot and heavy, and I guess I was angry he kept leading me on so I did the same back to him and tried to seduce him to sleep with me. He wouldn't. "So, do you know the reason why I came back to Interlaken?" I asked, as I got off the bed and walked to the other side of the room.

He said, "I know. I definitely have feelings for you and I'm so attracted to you."

I said, "No, I don't think you get it. Just listen to me and let me get this off my chest that I've held onto for six years. I've always had feelings for you, I thought we had a connection and I wanted to come back to see you and see if there was a possibility for us to be together. You can do what you please with what I'm saying to you."

He gave me a look like he felt sorry for me. He came over to me, gave me a hug, and kissed my forehead and said, "I don't know what to do, it's complicated." He was part of the reason why I fell in love with this place and I fell in love with his words and chose not to look at his actions.

This was happening again like it did when we first met back in 2008. I was angry and completely disappointed. I came all this way for him to lead me on, *again*. I wanted to leave my feelings in Switzerland with Matteo and move on. Matteo left my house and headed back home. I went back to the Mattenhof to find some of the Alpinraft guys who were always cool to me to grab some beers before I left. Matteo never reached out to say goodbye and we parted ways almost on similar terms all those years ago.

I had a couple more days left to enjoy before heading to Rimini, Italy. I had reached out to a hostel to inquire about managing their social media and be their photographer for events. I was at ease knowing I had a new place to visit and a new job lined up.

I was out on my porch and heard a group of guys nearby sitting outside their tents starting a fire for breakfast. I gave them a friendly wave and they called me over to join them. They introduced themselves: Adam, Gram, Woody, and Prof. (Professor). I never knew his real name. We talked about yoga and I told them I've been doing it for years. "Do you mind teaching us some after breakfast, we're going out for a climb. Do you want to join us on that as well? I have extra climbing gear," Adam said.

I told Adam, "I can totally teach you guys some yoga and I've never been climbing before, but I'm down to go." After we ate, the guys brought out their sleeping mats and laid them out in the grass. There was another girl and her friend nearby as well. I said, "If you ladies want to join, feel free, I'm going to teach yoga." I had never taught a "class" before but I played my yoga music my phone and went through a basic routine. I was giggling watching the guys struggle as they would mutter out, "How does she do that? I have to put my leg where? Oh fuck this shit, I'm too old." They did a great job for never doing it before but they told me they enjoyed it and thought my voice was super relaxing. Adam said, "Ok, great start to the morning and we're all stretched out for climbing, let's roll out."

Adam was convinced I'd have some natural ability to climb based on my yoga skills. We drove to another town called Unterseen where Adam knew of some good climbing spots. When we arrived ten minutes later, we grabbed the gear and snacks we brought. We hiked up a little bit into the mountains and found a beautiful white rock face that had to be at least thirty feet high. Gram walked over to me with his gear on, "I never climbed either." I told him I was relieved to hear that. Adam helped me put on my gear and said, "Alright, let's see what you got."

I looked back at Adam as I had to completely put my trust in this man to hold the other end of the rope. I climbed for the first time; each step and each move was carefully calculated. Climbing was like trying to solve a puzzle, trying to figure out where to put your foot or hand in the right pocket. I would get stuck at a spot not sure where to go, thinking, *I can't do this.* I looked down at Adam. He would encourage me to breathe and think. I took a deep breath and said to myself, "You got this." Eventually, when I slapped the chain at the top, I felt a rush of accomplishment. A sense of I can do anything I set my mind to.

I climbed five more times after that. Adam, who was holding my end of the rope, was impressed by how well I took to climbing being that it was my first time. He was surprised by the natural abilities I had and the techniques I used, which even some experienced climbers found difficult to do. He pushed me to see how I could handle each and every climb. He wanted to test my strength, both mentally and physically.

When I arrived at the hardest climb, I wasn't sure if I could do it. It was a lot of feet involved, which meant most of the climbing was done crawling up the rock. I tried to attempt it and slipped. It startled me. Adam said, "You're alright, I got you! Keep at it!" His encouragement and my drive to finish it kept me going. It took a lot of strength and control to climb to the top, I could feel the sweat beads rolling down my forehead as I used all the strength I had left in my legs to push myself up to grab the top of the rock and slap the chain. It was invigorating to say the least.

I looked back down at Adam and he screamed, "Ready?"

I said, "Climber ready," and he slowly rappelled me down the face of the mountain.

When my feet hit the ground, he gave me a high five and said, "You have no fear." Everything in that moment came in full circle for me because for so long fear has been the driving force of my anxiety. I felt like all the hard work I've done on myself was being validated and recognized. Gram said, "I'm beat, do you all fancy a celebratory beer?" After climbing all day, a nice cold beer is what we needed. We grabbed our gear, packed the car, and drove to the nearest pub. When we all sat down, we all let out a big sigh of relief.

Adam held up his beer and said, "Let's congratulate Laura on doing a killer job climbing today and you've become a new friend to us, we're happy you came out." We all held our beer glasses and cheered each other.

I said, "I can't thank you all enough, I really had a great time and I'm happy I met you all. This was a great way to end my trip here in Switzerland." Strangely, even though we spent most of the day together, I felt like I'd known them for a long time. Time in traveling is different. Time spans are usually shorter, but the time in between is deep and meaningful. You become closer faster than you would back home. The experiences you have with each other are enhanced because you don't have a lot of time together, which forces you to be present and enjoy what's in front of you in the short time you have. They wished me luck on my journey to Italy and said perhaps we'd see each other again.

On my final day, I started to miss the comforts of home and being around Americans. I went on a travel site called Couchsurfing, where you can host travelers. I was unable to host at the time since I had such a tiny home but I was able to hang out and show people around Interlaken. Two American girls named Alissa and Briana reached out to me and wrote me a message, "Oh my god, we're going to be in Interlaken tomorrow morning! Let's hang out."

I was supposed to leave tomorrow morning to Italy but I decided to hang out with them. I extended my time in Switzerland by a couple of days. I let the hostel owner in Rimini know that I was staying a little longer and would be there soon. He assured me not to worry and take my time.

They were about the same age as me and I started researching places I could take them. I arranged for us to go to the zipline park, where it had obstacles hanging up in the trees. I messaged them back, "I'll come get you from the train station in the morning and we'll come to where I live at The River Lodge. See you ladies soon!"

I was a little desperate for some girl time. It was difficult trying to fit in Interlaken, especially with the girls. Some were friendly towards me but others weren't. Some of the guys from Alpinraft said that they heard the girls were intimidated by me because I was pretty and a lot of the guys liked me. And to some of the guys, I felt like a dangling piece of meat. I felt alone during my time in Interlaken.

Anyway, late in the morning, I went to grab Alissa and Briana from the train station. I saw two girls with big backpacking packs and I ran up to them. "Alissa and Briana?" They were all smiles and ran towards me and gave me a big hug. I was so excited to have a little piece of home in Interlaken. I brought them back to my tiny home at The River Lodge to drop off their stuff and lock it in my house before going to the zipline park. We spent all day ziplining through the trees, Briana got stuck on one course because she chose the hard one and couldn't figure out the obstacle. Alissa and I were watching from afar on a different course laughing at her confusion but luckily she was rappelled down. We worked up an appetite and I said, "I'll cook you guys a barbeque back at the camp." We stuffed our faces with sausages, burgers and beers. I asked, "So where are you guys staying?" They told me Balmers Hostel, which was the other hostel down the street. Alissa asked, "So where are you going next?" I told them my plans to leave for Italy in a couple days. They looked at each other and said, "Oh my god, we're going to Italy too! We should go together."

I was happy to have some travel partners and I said, "Where could we go?" Briana said, "We should have a girl's trip in Cinque Terre. And then you can go to Rimini after." *How often do you get to do that?* I thought. I said, "Hell yes, let's do it."

Chapter 8: Why I Came Back to the U.S.

2014

"When you stand and share your story in an empowering way, your story will heal you, and your story will heal somebody else"- Iyanla Vanzant

I met up with Briana and Alissa outside their hostel and we trekked our way to the train for our eight-hour train ride to Cinque Terre. I had reached out to a hotel owner at La Francesca, which was a beautiful villa overlooking the sea. I mentioned I was a travel blogger and I would share my experience staying at his villa with my followers. Marco, the owner, was sweet and said he has plenty of travel bloggers come through and would love to have me stay. He said, "Bring your friends and I give you all the perfect room with the best view." The Villa is in the middle of the Cilento National Park, where it sits on the edge of a protected marine area stretching twenty kilometers down the coastline. We made sure we grabbed a bottle of Italian red wine to celebrate our three-day girl's trip and our new friendship. The views were breathtaking.

We walked out on our porch overlooking the sea and Alissa grabbed the wine and some glasses. We cheered, "To our girl's trip!"

***

And I said, "So now can we go, so I can find seafood?" I was completely deprived in Switzerland, as it was difficult to find and when I did it was expensive.

It was easy to get to the other towns; we hiked to every village during the course of our stay. Mainly because Briana was an energizer bunny when it came to hiking and walking everywhere. Alissa and I struggled to keep up at times, but we saw everything. The girls were obsessed with gelato. I laughed to myself as I write this because any gelato shop we passed they had to stop. I said, "I never had gelato." They turned their heads and gasped as if I had said the worst thing possible. "How dare you come to Italy and not have gelato. Now you must try it." I'm not going to lie, it was orgasmic. Everything was in Italy; the food was delicious to say the least. We spent the next two days hiking, eating, and drinking our way through Cinque Terre. Unfortunately, our time together was coming to a close where I had to head off to Rimini. I somehow miscalculated the days and had an extra day before I had to go to work. Briana and Alissa were excited to hang out for another day, "Come with us to Pisa! We're going there next and then to Rome, you're more than welcome to come there too." I didn't have plans and always wanted to see the Leaning Tower of Pisa.

When we arrived in Pisa, we stopped for lunch and were trying to figure out where we could stay. We were beyond exhausted from a long travel day and wanted to find a hostel that was closest to the train station so we could leave early the next morning. We found a hostel called Central Station Brandi's Guest House. It was in our price budget and it was five minutes from where we were eating. We started walking to the hostel and some guy on a vespa came up to us and asked, "Are you looking for the hostel?"

We said, "Yes."

He said, "Ok, great, I'm Carlo, I work there. I'll show you where it is." He sped away in the direction towards the hostel. We were sweating from carrying our heavy packs, and we slowly dragged our feet to follow him.

We walked in; it was very tiny, maybe one or two rooms with bunks. The walls were bright bubblegum pink. He said, "I do not have any more room for you ladies, but I have another hostel back near the train station." We were exhausted and annoyed we had to walk back to the train station but we did anyway and met him at the fountain in the middle of the town. He was initially a little flirty with Briana when we first got there, which was weird but not so much where we felt unsafe. We stood at the fountain and saw Carlo driving towards us on his vespa. He stopped and asked, "So who wants to ride on the back?" Me and Alissa were in a mood and had too much to carry. Briana hopped on the back without hesitation. They sped off. *This was when I slowly started to question what we were getting ourselves into.*

Carlo took us to the other hostel. It was inside an apartment building. We walked inside; it looked like someone's flat. It's not uncommon for people to use their homes as hostels or guesthouses, so I wasn't too alarmed. We went into the room where there were three bunks; some looked like other people were staying there too. Carlo said, "There's four other English girls staying in the other room down the hall." Alissa and Briana were unaware of my suspicion but knowing there were other girls down the hall made me feel more at ease. He said, "Okay 45 Euro for all three of you."

I told the girls I'd pay for them and they can pay me back later. I said to Carlo, "I only have a 50. Do you have change?"

He said, "No problem, I'll bring you downstairs where we can get change."

I walked with him to fill out necessary paperwork to stay at the hostel; he shut the door where Briana and Alissa were unpacking. We were standing in the middle of the hallway filling out the paperwork, showing him my passport. I don't know if he was impressed or turned on that I had an Italian passport. He said, "Do you speak Italian?"

I said, "No." He was probably about 6ft tall, 250lbs. He was a big guy compared to me and I'm 5'2, so out of nowhere he picked me up to where I was bear hugging him from the front. He said, "Kiss me." I was startled and tried to wiggle my body out of his tight grip. I moved my head when he tried to kiss me. Every time I moved my head, he moved in again to kiss me. I gave him a quick peck because I felt like I didn't have any choice and I wanted to get down. I said, "I just want my change, would you hurry up already!" I was pissed at this point. I didn't find him attractive at all and mix that with exhaustion and hunger, you can imagine my attitude towards Carlo.

He said, with an animalistic sexual stare, "Look what you do to me." I noticed a bulge in his pants.

I was starting to get angry and lose my patience. We had a long day of traveling and I said, "I didn't do shit to you, just get me my damn change."

We went to walk downstairs to get my change when we he threw me against the wall in a dark corner of the hallway. You think you would know what to do in a dangerous situation. I can't tell you how many times a situation like this had gone through my head, or stories I've heard, I would always tell myself I'd kill someone if they attacked me or at the very least fight back.

***

I was caught off guard and I froze. He was feeling me up, touching my chest over my clothes and I was trying to push him away. He unzipped his pants and took my hand to touch his genitals. I said stop probably about four times. I grabbed his hand because he was trying to go up my shorts. He grabbed my wrist and slammed against the wall behind me.

That was the moment where I was really scared. I felt his strength against mine and knew it would be hard to fight him off if I had to. I'm sure you're thinking, "Why didn't you scream?" Everything happened so fast. Scared, in shock, and it was hard to think.

On the fifth time of me telling him to stop, he finally did. I took my hand to face palm him and push him away from me. He looked at me in disgust and said, "I hate you."

I said, "Get the fuck outta here, you're a pig. Go get my fucking change."

When we came back upstairs to see Briana and Alissa, Carlo and I stood in the doorway. The girls were chatting with Carlo about where the tower was. He was hugging me from the side and acted like nothing happened. The girls were smiling and laughing with Carlo and one thing about me is, I can't hide my emotions. It's usually written all over my face. Briana was laughing at something Carlo said and I kept staring at her. She would catch my eye and go back to talking but I kept looking at her. She caught my eye again and then she caught on and realized something was wrong. Carlo left; I put a table in front of the door because we didn't have locks. I told them what happened. Both of their jaws dropped in shock. We went to look for those other English girls down the hall. We all walked together and the door was locked. We peeked through the keyhole and I just saw suitcases, but the room didn't look used at all. I thought, *This doesn't seem right, I don't think there were ever any other people here.* I started looking around the other rooms. The other one looked like someone's bedroom. It had a TV, microwave, and an IV bag pole. Any red flags I had were waving and I was on high alert. I was convinced there had to be drugs somewhere.

I was shaking and trying not to cry. I felt violated and disgusted; I went straight to the bathroom to wash my hands. I wanted to wash away what had just happened and the stench on my hands from his dirty balls. There wasn't any soap; I almost used a whole bottle of hand sanitizer to clean my hands. The girls' eyes were widened with fear. They said, "What do we do now?"

I said, "We pack our shit and get the fuck outta here. This is not a safe place. I'd rather pay 200.00 Euro and know we're safe than stay here."

We immediately packed our things and left for another hostel. We found a safer chain hostel further away from the train station. We checked in and got to our room; it was private and it was just us. We stood there for a moment to process everything. We still had our bottle of nice Italian red wine from Cinque Terre. I said, "Let's open this."

As I poured the wine into tiny plastic cups, they said, "What are we cheering for?"

I said holding back tears, "Let's cheers to the fact that we are safe and that shit could have been a lot worse." We cheered our wine cups together and gave each other a big hug. After a few more glasses of wine, we were talking about what happened and it made us even more angry. We all were broke and I was worried about the 45.00 Euro I lost since I was running low on cash. We collectively decided go back and find Carlo to get our money back. All three of us walked together to the first hostel, and we found him. We said, "Give us our money back."

He tried to fight us on it, "No refunds."

We said, "The hostel was dirty and disgusting." Which it was. We didn't talk about what happened to me because we didn't think we would get our money back that way. I know that sounds insane, but we all were running low on funds and the principle of him doing what he did to me and how he treated us pissed us off. He gave us the money back and we left.

I had backlash after writing about this on my travel blog. People responded, "Why didn't you call the police?" For one, I didn't know the police number in Italy. And two, I wanted us to get out of there safe. Safety was my main priority. If I could go back in time, I would have gone to the police. I later contacted the hostel website to report his hostel, and they contacted the proper authorities but nothing came of it.

After Pisa, it was time for Briana, Alissa, and myself to part ways. They were heading to Rome, and I had a job lined up in Rimini. We hugged each other tight, exchanged contact information to stay in touch, and wished each other safe travels. And that was it. We had gone through a lot in the last couple of weeks. In some strange way, I was glad that what happened to me did while we were together. I had to go back to survival mode. Now I was traveling solo again. I wasn't able to fully emotionally process what happened to me in Pisa, I had to put it in the back of my mind and focus on finding my way to Rimini. At this point, I was growing tired of traveling. I felt like I kept getting the short end of the stick wherever I went.

I eventually found the hostel in Rimini, which was right near the beach. I began working for them to manage their social media page and bring traffic to their website and hostel. I also did their photography for their famous pub crawls throughout the town. I was feeling quite uneasy from not knowing what to do or how I was going to make this work. I didn't realize this hostel was a huge party hostel, which was not the scene I wanted to be in again. Rimini was like the Interlaken of Italy. I was beginning to worry about money because the Euro wasn't strong and I could see it draining my account faster than when I was living in Switzerland.

I found myself in a similar situation at The River Lodge. I asked the owner when I would get paid and he said I wouldn't. I guess the language barrier and miscommunication via our messages got lost in translation. He said, "You work free, you stay free." I thought, *Fuck. Not this again.* In a slight panic, I thought about running to Thailand or India where it was cheaper but I wasn't sticking around long enough to wait for the visa process to go through.

I was emotional and feeling defeated. I called my dad because he always gives it to me straight. I told him what happened in Pisa and he was upset as any father would be to hear their daughter was sexually assaulted. He told me, "Come home and find work." Hearing that was like a stab to my heart. My pride rose up because coming home in my mind meant I failed. My dad said, "You can still travel, but it's best you come home, regroup, and figure out what you're going to do." As heartbroken as I was to think about coming home, a part of me was relieved. I hadn't mentally and emotionally processed Pisa, and I was starting to miss home anyway. I had money to last me a few months, but I didn't want to go until my last dollar and be in a shittier situation of not being able to get home. So, I reluctantly decided to fly back home to the states.

Chapter 9: Pura Vida?

2014

"I have found out that there ain't no surer way to find out whether you like people or hate them than to travel with them."--Mark Twain, Tom Sawyer Abroad

Mark messaged me and asked, "Have you heard about what happened to Adam?" I hadn't spoken to Mark in a while since Costa Rica and said, "No, we had a falling out towards the end of the trip and never spoke again." Mark was taking a while to answer me, and my heart was beginning to race and expect the worst. Mark said, "He passed away." My heart sank with sadness and then guilt. Our tiffs were getting bad towards the end of our trip, and we began staying in separate hostels. When you travel with someone for a long period of time and spend 24/7 with each other, whether you know the person well or not, it's almost inevitable fights will arise. I felt horrible because I wanted to reach out to him after Costa Rica but I wasn't sure if he would answer me or accept my apology. And now it was too late.

I asked Mark, "Do you know what happened?"

Mark said, "I don't know, I assume maybe it was a skydiving accident. But don't quote me." I went to check Facebook but noticed Adam and I were not friends. I couldn't remember if he deleted me or if I deleted him. As I was going through his public posts he had from our trip two years ago, old feelings were coming back, and I realized it might have been me who deleted him, which made me feel even worse. Our fights were so silly now that I think back to it. Not even worth getting so upset over but shit happens, right? And plus, you don't really expect someone to die two years later. I've been holding off writing this chapter because I don't know how to go about telling the story of our trip together. If Adam could read this, I'd say I'm sorry for the bad blood we had and wished we had worked it out sooner.

To preface the rest of the chapter, I want everyone to know how great of a person Adam was. I'd compare our arguments to sibling fights and at the time they seemed to be a lot worse from spending a lot of time together. So, I will admit, I took some things more personally than I should have. Regardless of what happened during our trip, Adam taught me a lot about traveling, rock climbing, and also about myself. I will always appreciate him for that.

Adam was a good-looking guy, spikey hair with a dishy Australian accent. We had a great time in Switzerland when I went rock climbing with him and his friends. I reached out to Adam asking when we'd go climbing together again. Adam and I skyped for weeks trying to figure out where to go. I asked, "Where is good climbing?" Adam said, "We could do Canada or Costa Rica?" I said, "Costa Rica would be nice, I've never been there." Adam said, "I'll make an itinerary and look up good climbing spots." We planned to rent a car and hop around to each city we wanted to see. Both of us also knew that our itinerary would not be set in stone.

During our Skype sessions, I told Adam, "So this trip is strictly platonic and there wouldn't be any romance."

Adam said, "That's not a problem." I guess being naive, I took him for his word.

The night before I had to fly out, I fell ill. I felt like I got hit by a truck, high fever and couldn't get out of bed. My dad came upstairs to check on me, "Are you sure you still want to go? Maybe you should cancel." I had already paid for the flight and I had my herbal remedies strong enough to kick it out. I got in touch with Adam to let him know how shitty I felt but I was still coming. Flying isn't fun to begin with and it's even worse when you're sick. When I finally arrived after a stop-over in Florida. I found my bag with the rest of the checked luggage, and I noticed a strange smell. I honestly wasn't sure if it was my bag or someone else's. I was exhausted and still feverish. I finally saw Adam, and when I walked outside it was humid as hell. He gave me a puppy dog sad face and said, "Oh you poor thing." He grabbed my bag and said, "Well I'm glad you made it. I already have our hotel set up and got the rental car."

He asked, "What is that smell?"

I said, "Shit, you can smell it too? I have no idea! It smelled after I picked it up at the baggage claim." It smelled like rancid beer. The car Adam rented was a manual. I said, "I thought you were gonna get an automatic so we can split the driving?"

He said, "I tried, but almost all the cars here are manual." Adam was stuck with the driving but he didn't care. He got plenty of car insurance so he can drive as wild as he could. We tried to find out how to get a SIM card for our phones at some local phone store. I don't know why this tended to happen, but when I travel, usually on the first day I get a lot of anxiety. But I was also sick and I was overwhelmed being in a new place and just wanted to sleep.

I remember standing in the phone store with Adam and I felt anxious. I told him, "Do you mind if I step outside for a minute to get some air?" I took a few deep breaths, tears welling up in eyes, and tried to calm down.

Adam walked outside, "You alright?" I tried hiding my tears and wiped them away from my eyes.

Adam said, "Aw, you're alright. You just don't feel good. Don't worry, I'll handle the phones. Go sit in the car and we'll go straight to the hotel after this." A few minutes later he came out to the car, "I got us GPS as well, so we don't get lost."

I said, "That's always good."

Adam pulled into this hotel not too far from where we were, and I said, "Why are we staying here? I thought we were staying on a budget."

Adam said, "You're not feeling well. I'll get us a nice room so you can relax and rest up for our drive tomorrow."

I said, "Thank you so much, I really appreciate it. I'll split it with you."

He said, "Don't worry about it." I didn't have the energy to argue but he knew I was grateful. I started to unpack some of my things and noticed the strange smell seeped into my bag and my clothes were smelly too. I packed detergent packets and ran the tub to wash some of my clothes. I threw my bag in there too, to soak it in detergent. It helped the smell. I think someone had something in their bag and it leaked onto mine. After all the washing, I showered and then crashed for a few hours. Adam gently woke me up and asked, "How are you feeling? Are you hungry? Want to grab some dinner? There's a place nearby we can walk to." I felt a bit better, but still had a slight fever. It was a nice seafood restaurant, and again, Adam was being sweet and paid for our meals. I was happy I had an appetite.

I said, "Would you stop paying for things, we're supposed to split it." He insisted it was fine.

Shortly after dinner, I went back to the room and crashed for the rest of the night. We woke up early the next morning and headed towards Alajuela. We stayed at a campsite where our first climbing spot would be, but we had to hike in to our sleeping area. I barely complained out loud, but in my head I was thinking, *I'm still not 100% and we have to hike?!* We could only drive to the opening of the wilderness and had to take as much gear as we could carry on our backs. Surprisingly, when we finally arrived at our camp spot, I felt dramatically better. I said to Adam, "I think I needed to sweat it out."

He was ahead of me on the trail and said, "Good shit! Let's keep going then, we're almost there." I loved where we were staying. It was along the river and surrounded nature, where we slept outside. The landowner gave us crappy mattresses to sleep on, but I had a single tent and Adam just had a sleeping bag and sleeping mat. We took the mattresses anyway and made it work. I hadn't used my tent and, of course, the first time I set it up, it broke. I slept in a dilapidated tent but it had a mesh roof where I could see the stars. The moon was so bright I had to sleep with my sweater over my eyes. Nature was singing her sweet lullaby. I heard the river moving and small animals making their nightly noises. Slowly, my eyes grew heavy, and I slept like a baby.

We walked maybe a foot or two to where we were sleeping to climb the rocks. Adam said, "This is a bit harder than what we did in Switzerland but I'm curious as to how you'll do." Adam went first with ease. He had a beautiful technique and made it to the top. I remembered how much I loved watched him climb. I could tell he was in his element and completely lost in the moment. It was my turn, and I made it to the top mostly from his encouragement. He told me, "You definitely have a natural talent for climbing." Coming from such a seasoned climber, I was flattered. After a long day of climbing, we hiked up to the town to grab some food to make a barbeque and blissfully enjoyed where we were and how beautiful this place was.

The next morning, we hiked our way out of the camp. We reached a gate and it was locked. We couldn't get out. There was a number I was able to make out. "Adam, do you have any cell service?"

Adam looked at his phone and said, "Nope, not a single bar. And my phone is dying." My phone was already dead.

I said, "Try to call the number and see if anyone picks up to get someone here to unlock the gate. I know some Spanish but I'm a little better at understanding than speaking. My brain went completely blank as to how to say, "Open the gate."

After sitting there for an hour or so, I thought we'd be stuck here. We had limited supplies and water from our last food run the other day. The landowner eventually came, and we were relieved. When we got to our car, we headed towards La Paz Waterfalls and got unbelievably lost. The GPS cut out and we were driving for hours. We stopped at a gas station to ask if we were headed in the right direction, and we couldn't get an answer. It was dark and hard to see, plus the roads were dangerous. The roads were straight dirt roads on the side of a mountain without any street lights. I said, "Adam, we need to stop. We can't see shit and we have no idea where we are. Let's try again in the morning."

Adam agreed and found a taxi driver who was willing to lead us the way to a hotel in the nearest town. I think I knocked out in 2.5 seconds. Adam joked the next morning and said he never saw anyone who could fall asleep that fast before.

We woke up at 5:00 a.m. to start our day early with the sun so we could see where we were going. For some strange reason, waking up at 5:00 a.m. became the norm for us. The sunlight looked like noon at 5:00 a.m. It was so bright out you couldn't sleep in. And also, we'd on average had fifteen-hour days traveling and doing things. Finally, we made it to the waterfalls, and it was worth getting lost for hours the night before. Lesson learned, we should drive during the day to new cities. The butterfly sanctuary was my favorite. As you walked in, there was relaxing spa music playing as butterflies flew all around you. I had to tiptoe my way around the place because I didn't want to step on any of them. The butterflies landed on me as I walked by, and I even had one land on me perfectly on my finger.

After a few hours at the waterfalls, we drove to our next destination. While on the way, we drove through a town similar to Interlaken. It had lots of extreme adventure sports and looked like a cool backpacker town. I suggested we should stay there and it was a five-star backpacker hostel. They had glamping tents outside and dorm style rooms. There was a big pool, a couple bars, and slacklining over the pool. Adam wanted to stay in the glamping tents, but we'd have to share a bed.

I said, "Let's stay in the dorms to meet people."

He was annoyed and said, "I don't want to deal with drunk backpackers. I understood but I felt like there was a slight ulterior motive for him wanting to share a bed with me because he wouldn't budge.

I said, "We're the only ones there and it'd be fun to meet other travelers plus the dorms are cheaper." Adam was insistent. I said, "You can sleep there if you want, I'll go into the dorms." He wouldn't even agree to that. I was beginning the process to pay for my dorm and he eventually changed his mind to stay in the dorms too.

We heard there were hot springs in the area, and we didn't want to go to the man-made ones. One of our roommates overheard there was a local spot not too far from the hostel. We introduced ourselves. Jamie was a British girl traveling alone, and we offered for her to come with us. Sometimes it's nice to add a new person to the mix when you've been with the same person for a long time.

When I travel it's like a little kid experiencing something for the first time. Even the littlest things excite me. We walked by some locals outside the hostel and asked some locals, "Donde esta la Hot Springs?" The locals pointed us in the direction, which was only a five minute walk. We hiked along a trail and could hear people talking, laughing and rushing water. We found the natural hot spring. Sitting in the hot spring, it was actually hot. I found it fascinating the volcano in the distance was warming up the water. The spring was filled with volcanic rocks and, of course, I had to take one as a souvenir. How often do you get to hold a real volcanic rock?

When we got back to our room, we had a new roommate. He was bunking on top of my bunk. He introduced himself to us, "Hi, I'm Mark." He was an attractive guy with a great smile. He was from Montreal, Canada. He told us he just came back from Liberia. At the time, Ebola just broke out and some people were nervous to travel. When he said Liberia, I thought, *holy shit, he was just in Liberia where the outbreak was and he's sleeping above me.* Later, I told him, he laughed his ass off. "No, Liberia, Costa Rica." I laughed in relief. We met other guys too, from The Netherlands, and we all became close quickly. As a dorm, we all went out to a festival in town to dance and have drinks. I tapped out eventually while the rest of the boys continued. I went back to the hostel and around 5:00 a.m., I felt my bed shake. I awoke to Mark sitting on the corner of my bed. Half asleep, I whispered, "What are you doing?"

All he said was, "Hi." in a slurred tone, smiled, and said, "I'm taking off my shoes." I smiled back and went to sleep. Because he was cute, I let that slide.

Mark and Adam took a liking to each other, they formed a bromance and after their night out they decided to go rafting until noon, still drunk off their asses. I woke up not knowing where they went and didn't realize they came back to the hostel and went back out again, according to my roommates. I was kind of annoyed because I didn't want to stay at the hostel another night, and 11:00 a.m. was only time to tell the front desk if you were staying another night, and of course, I couldn't get a hold of Adam so I paid for another night. When they got back to the hostel, Adam said, "I invited Mark and Jamie to travel with us and head to the ocean." The boys wanted to surf and us girls would have drinks and sunbathe on the beach. I was secretly delighted Mark was coming with us. I wanted to get to know him more.

We arrived at the ocean. The air was fresh and tasted like salt water, the breeze was just right, and the temperature was hot but not humid at all. We found a hostel right on the beach in Tamarindo. The Coral Reef is a backpacker's hostel with bright colored walls and multiple hammocks in the common area. Jeff was the owner and he also owned the restaurant attached to the hostel where he was bringing North Carolina barbeque to Costa Rica. The food was mouthwatering and it was always great to meet other Americans around the world. Jeff's hospitality was admirable. One night, Mark and I were having dinner and wanted a bottle of wine. Jeff didn't have the one I wanted on hand and said, "Don't worry about it, I will go to the store right now and grab you a bottle."

I told Jeff, he doesn't have to go through all that trouble. I'll get something else. Jeff insisted. And I was pleasantly surprised how he would go above and beyond for the people who stayed at his hostel.

***

Mark and I took the bottle and went to sit on the beach. Drunk with lust, we sat with the sand between our toes looking at the sunset. We laughed and enjoyed *Pura Vida*, which Costa Ricans hold dear to their hearts. In English it simply translates to "Pure Life, but in Costa Rica it's deeper than that, it's a lifestyle. Mark leaned in and kissed me. We walked holding our flip flops and headed back to the room. We all were sharing a four-bed dorm and would hide the key above a painting on the wall near our door. Mark and I made love in our drunken state, and I honestly couldn't tell you how good it was or not. I was starting to realize even though the lust and feelings I had for him, were only temporary. I was getting tired of having temporary flings. In my search for love, I was going about it the wrong way. I kind of always felt being a traveler meant I couldn't have a real relationship.

In my mind, I started to overanalyze and think of how Mark and I could work. I did that a lot with men I liked or slept with quickly. *I would make the effort to see him. I'd go above and beyond for someone. Why can't this work?* I wouldn't mind traveling to Montreal or even move there if things went in that direction. But when you travel together, as I mentioned earlier, the concept of time is different because you get closer much faster than you would at home. *But why would I make all the effort for someone who wouldn't do the same for me?* Thoughts of Damien, Dominik and Matteo began running through my head. Why was I doing this to myself? Something needed to change.

I met Adam at a local club later that night and he was pretty intoxicated. At this point in our trip, he was getting on my last nerve. He'd party so hard the night before doing god knows what kind of drugs, allegedly from what Mark told me, and he wasn't able to drive to the next destination because he was still fucked up. I said, "Why would you get that fucked up knowing we had to be outta here early in the morning to go to our next spot?" He was on a long binge of partying and not sleeping, which pissed me off because I didn't want to get in the car with him like that. Adam scoffed, took another sip of his drink, and tried to pull me in to dance. I wasn't having it. I walked to the other side of the club to get away from him. A few moments later, Adam walked up behind me and grabbed my waist.

I turned around and said, "What are you doing?"

He was slurring his words and said, "You look like you're in pain from Mark rejecting you."

Confused and caught off guard, I said, "What are you talking about?"

"I don't know, you look heartbroken."

I told him, "You're drunk and you're not making any sense." All of sudden, we heard a bunch of glasses breaking to the right of us and guys yelling. The security told us we all had to leave because fights kept breaking out and it wasn't safe.

Adam said, "I'll walk with you back to the hostel to be safe." We walked down the streets together not saying a word.

When we arrived at our room, I told Adam I was going to stay up for a little bit, write in my travel journal and go to bed. Adam started to say something but stopped.

I could sense his emotions, "What were you about to say Adam?"

He said, "Nothing, I'm just disappointed you and I didn't hook up."

I didn't respond as I didn't know what to say.

"Mark and I talked earlier and he told me the conversation you two had. Where he told you he didn't want anything more than just hooking up with you."

I said, "It is what it is."

Mark and I kept going back and forth between having tension and being flirty. Adam, Mark, and I all went out for karaoke. It's not my thing but I went anyway, it was a lot of fun all three of us singing together. Mark ditched me and went to hang out with Adam. I asked, "Can I join?"

Mark said, "No. It's boys' night." I rolled my eyes and continued to drink the rest of my beer. Adam was adamant about finding a woman to sleep with. He'd hit on women at the bar and with his luck they all had boyfriends. Adam grew frustrated. And looking back I can see why he was jealous of Mark and I getting together. I didn't notice his envy because I thought with our growing tension, he wouldn't want to be near me at all. I left them to their boys' night and told them to have a fun. I went back to our room, which had one queen-sized bed and one bunk bed. Adam and Jamie shared the bunk, Mark and I shared the queen bed. I was fast asleep and I felt Mark cuddling up next to me. He tried to kiss me. I said, "Ew, Jesus Christ, did you throw up and try to kiss me?"

He was startled by my reaction and said, "No, I did have nachos though."

We both died laughing and I kicked him out of bed and said, "Will ya go brush your damn teeth." Mark made me laugh constantly, and I hated the love/hate relationship we had. The mixed messages Mark was sending were starting to get to me, but this time I tried to remind myself to not have any expectations with him.

Adam decided we were going to spend the rest of the trip in Tamarindo. I had about a week left. Jamie and Mark were going to leave us soon, too. Jamie had to head to Nicaragua to meet up with her boyfriend, and Mark had to meet up with his brother in another city. Again, Adam didn't consult me about staying in Tamarindo. I was annoyed. This wasn't just his trip and I knew he wanted to surf and party. I said, "Well, I don't want to stay the rest of my time here in

Tamarindo. You're staying longer than me. I'd like to finish our itinerary."

He said, "Fine, we'll stay till Friday and then head to Montezuma to see the waterfalls and then be in San Jose, Costa Rica by Sunday." We agreed in the beginning of the trip that he'd dropped me back off in San Jose at the airport since he was staying in Costa Rica longer, and I had to go back home.

Jamie left the next morning, and it was sad to see her go. The boys went surfing, and I was going to find a way to Santa Teresa to stay at a yoga hostel. I didn't believe Adam wanted to leave by Friday and I figured I should just go off on my own. When the boys came back, Mark and I went to go have some pizza and drinks on the beach and watch the thunderstorm roll in. We then went back to the hostel to lie in the hammocks and read books in the common area. Adam was talking to other people in the hostel while Mark and I squeezed into one hammock, as they were big enough for two people. He was reading his book and I was slowly being swayed to sleep until I saw someone with some authentic empanadas similar to how my dad made them. I said, "Oh my god, are those Argentinian empanadas?"

The guy said, "Yeah they are." And pointed out where I could get them across the street.

I was sitting on the edge of Mark's hammock, I turned to him and asked, "Have you ever had one?" He said he didn't. I said, "You gotta try it. Want to come with me?" Adam, out of nowhere said, "Well if that isn't a big fuck you."

I said, "What are you talking about?" I knew he was pissed I asked Mark but it wasn't like he couldn't come with us. I said, "You can come with us, it's not a big deal."

He was angry and responded, "Oh, and they say you can never hit a woman." I could feel the heat rise into my cheeks as they turned red. I was so angry and embarrassed as he said this in front of everyone in the common area.

I said, "Wow, is this trip almost over?"

He shot right back at me, "It can be."

I looked at Mark and mouthed, "I have to take a walk."

He said, "Want me to come with you?" We walked away from Adam as he sat back with the rest of the people. I was holding back angry tears. Mark caressed my shoulders, "You're okay. That was fucked up of him to say. You guys have some real tension building, you can always say something to him about it."

I didn't see the point. I said, "I don't see the sense of talking to someone who won't get it."

The next day, Mark had to leave us and meet up with his brother in Nicaragua. Mark told me, "Come wait with me at the bus stop?" We walked over at the bench to wait for his bus. We talked, laughed, and as I turned my head to look the other direction I could see the bus coming down the street. My smile wasn't as big anymore and I tried to mask my sadness with faking a smile. We exchanged numbers, "Let's stay in touch," he said. I agreed but I knew we wouldn't. He kissed me one last time, and hopped on the bus. I've become numb at saying goodbye to people I've met. I've learned to push the emotions to the side and move on.

One of the Dutch guys from our dorm room and a travel blogger from Spain, Adam met while he was surfing, was now coming with us to Santa Teresa. Adam's decision. The Spanish girl, Priscilla, needed a ride to Santa Teresa, so it was more practical for Adam to drop us both off and he could go off on his own. When we arrived in Santa Teresa, I thought he would drop us off and go. "I'm going to stay here too," Adam said. I didn't want to anywhere near him. We were not speaking at this point. I was worried he booked the same hostel as me, but luckily, him, the Dutch guy and Priscilla were staying at another hostel ten minutes down the street. I grabbed my things from the car and walked to the yoga hostel, but they were unfortunately all booked for that night. They said to come back in the morning and recommended for me to stay across the street at another hostel. I wanted to be alone. I needed a break from Adam, plus I was bummed Mark left.

I went to have dinner alone with a beautiful glass of Malbec (my favorite) and tried to enjoy my last couple days here. I could hear Adam's voice from down the street. I turned around and saw them walking towards my table. He and the others sat with me. I was glaring at him drinking my wine. He said, "This is where our hostel recommended for us to eat." I entertained them sitting there but I could sense the other people noticed our tension. I started to ask about how I'd get back to San Jose from here. Adam seemed to change his tune about taking me back. He said, "We could leave Monday morning." I was fuming. My flight was leaving Monday.

I said, "I'd rather not do that since it's a six and a half hour drive from here, the roads suck, and our GPS hasn't been reliable."

He said, "Well, I can teach you how to drive the car back." I thought, *Oh sure, that's great. Teach me how to drive stick in one to two days to drive back without a GPS, with crazy Costa Rican drivers and horrible roads.* I left the table before I flipped out on him. Our agreement was we'd head south from where we were so we could drive to the ferry and bring the car back to San Jose. Adam obviously had other plans. Now I was stranded in Santa Teresa, left to figure out how to get to San Jose by Monday to make my flight.

I called my friend Carter who was a travel agent from back home because I was upset and didn't know what to do. Prior to leaving for Costa Rica, Carter and I went on a couple dates. Carter said, "You need to figure out a plan B. I can look up the map for you and try to figure it out with the travel agent software I have."

I said, "That would be so helpful, thank you!"

"I'll email you what I find."

I said, "Thanks, and I'm going to go now. I had a long frustrating day."

The next morning, I met two travelers from Canada from my dorm room. They asked if they could join me for breakfast. I said, "Sure." I asked, "Hey do you know any way to get to San Jose from here because I have to leave Monday."

The owner of the hostel overheard our discussion and said, "You won't make it out by bus because buses don't come here. However, there are regional flights that fly right to San Jose airport."

***

Later on, I bumped into Adam and told him what I was doing. He said, "That's perfect, brilliant plan." His lack of concern to help me only pissed me off even more. He said, "We're going to Montezuma to see the waterfalls." I wanted to go so I swallowed my pride and went with them. On the way there, we were starving and stopped at a little local soda. Sodas are small local restaurants, and the food was usually delicious and cheap. The hike in spot was across the street and we met our guide. He said we could pay to help us to get to the falls, but Adam didn't want him. He wasn't expensive, maybe ten to twenty bucks. The guide kept saying hiking without a guide is dangerous, but it is doable. I didn't want to take the chance and said, "Let's get him, it'll make it easier, and it's not expensive." Thank the damn lord we did because it was not easy at all. Plus, the danger of flash floods was real and it had recently rained, which caused the rapids to be intense to walk through.

The guide said, "Everyone must listen to me if he notices a flash flood coming." I was uneasy. The rocks in the water were slippery and I had flip flops on. The guide said I could leave my shoes on the trail and grab them on the way back. The guide was hiking barefoot so I figured it might be easier. It made a difference, and I liked walking through the mud and have the mud slide in between my toes. The waterfalls were beautiful, and the water was rushing more intensely because of the recent rain. We all sat and appreciated the beauty and thanked our guide for taking us to see the falls.

We headed back to our separate hostels, I did a night yoga class before bed and fell sweetly into bed. Carter had texted me and woke me. He wanted to chat because he was feeling down. I told him I'd be up for a small chat. We had a deep conversation, and we discussed my brother and his addiction issues. Carter told me his ex-girlfriend had similar problems. We realized we had more in common than we thought, but I said, "I'm sorry to cut you short, let's chat about this tomorrow when I'm more awake."

Carter said, "No worries, get your rest."

***

The next morning, I did morning yoga and ate luscious fruit and drank tea with some girls from my dorm. I went to walk around town and met some guy who owned a surf shop. He suggested I should go surfing with him. I wasn't keen on surfing--the ocean kind of freaks me out. When I got back to the hostel, he messaged me and said, "There's a girl from Los Angeles going and they need one more person." I figured I'd try it since Costa Rica is known for their waves.

When I got there, I met Karine. She was a fun girl from Israel but recently moved to Los Angeles. We went to Playa Hermosa, and the waves weren't too bad. I was able to get up three or four times, but I definitely got tossed around a bit. Karine and I were in the water waiting for waves and she was telling me about Israel and about the birthright trip. I told her, "I always wanted to go to Israel and do my birthright trip."

She said, "I work for them so let me know when you want to go, I'll help you with the application process."

After surfing, we had a couple drinks and a much needed dinner. We exchanged information to stay in touch. She continued telling me everything about Israel. And Israel was becoming more intriguing.

***

I hadn't seen Adam all day and the next day I was leaving to go back home. I thought, *Wow, he's not even going to say bye.* But I guess I wasn't even surprised. I was happy I was leaving on a good note, from staying at the yoga hostel and surfing with Karine. The next morning, I was about to head out and realized I forgot some of my things in the car. I asked the hostel manager if I could borrow a bike really fast to go down the road. I biked as fast as I could down to Adam's hostel and asked, "Hey, I left some of my things in the car, can I grab it?"

All he said was, "We have to figure out money." Money we owed each other. I found it funny, he was now asking me for money for things he insisted on paying for in the beginning.

I said, "Yeah sure." But thought, *He's not getting shit for how he treated me and left me without a way to get back to the airport.* Adam then asked, "I have a layover in NYC. Would you take me around when I get there?" I was speechless he would even ask me being we've been at each other's throats. I didn't respond and grabbed my things.

I took the shuttle to the town of Tambor where the little plane would fly into San Jose. I met Tammy who was from Florida and came here to visit her daughter who was living here. She was bright, wearing lots of bohemian colors and jewelry.After we got to talking, I found out her ex-husband lived in my town back in NJ. I thought, *How funny, what a small world.* The little plane arrived, and man was it small. We and our luggage had to be weighed to see how much could fit on the plane. I've heard many stories of those tiny planes crashing, so I wasn't exactly thrilled to fly. I'm petite, 5'2, and my head almost hit the ceiling of the plane, so you can imagine how small it was. Tammy sat next to me, and we found out we were on the same flight back to Florida; my first stop. The flight to the airport was beautiful, and a little scary because you could feel the turbulence a lot more in a small plane.

Carter insisted he pick me up from the airport. I reminded him I was not looking my prettiest, I had two weeks worth of bug spray on with my hair in a messy bun and was wearing the least of my dirty clothes. He said, "I don't care. See you soon."

When I arrived home, it was reverse culture shock. I was initially excited to be home and to see Carter, but I guess being in the jungle for two weeks and being away from civilization, I was anxious from the overstimulation. Carter was there to meet me at the baggage claim with roses, he was dressed nicely, and my feelings for him were different. Everything was too much all at once. When we got to his car, he said, "Why are you so quiet?"

I said, "It's been a long travel day, I'm just tired." When I walked closer to his car, I noticed he had decorated his car with a welcome home banner and balloons. It was sweet, but something about it was disingenuous. I was almost in tears in the car, and he asked, "What's wrong?" I said, "I want to go back to Costa Rica, if I'd booked a one-way ticket, I would have stayed longer."

I stopped writing this chapter up until this point. Reliving my Costa Rica trip with Adam saddened me with grief. I felt horrible how we left things and I never got to truly apologize and let him know it's water under the bridge. I wasn't even sure if Adam would like me writing about our trip. I found his family contacts on his facebook page since he had that section open to the public. I reached out to his mother and explained who I was and how terribly sorry I was for her loss. My message to her was as follows:

Hi Adam's mom,

You don't know me but I am a friend of Adam's. Hearing of his passing the other day has been on my mind quite a bit and has been bothering me. We met in Switzerland when I moved there on a whim at a campsite with a bunch of his buddies. He immediately, with open arms, invited me to come rock climbing with them. I accepted without even knowing your son at all. I trusted him despite being strangers and literally having someone hold the other end of the rope with your life on the line. He taught me a lot in a short period of time and even praised me on my natural ability. He showed me the ropes, so to speak. I remember watching him climb and he trusted me to belay him. Granted, this was my first time climbing and belaying but I caught on quick. I was in awe of his passion for climbing. He was a different person when he climbed. You can tell there was a fire there and it was beautiful to watch.

A short time after I wound up heading back home to the states but Adam and I kept in touch. We wanted to climb again together and I was itching to travel again and we enjoyed our time climbing so we did a spontaneous road trip to Costa Rica for two weeks, well for him much longer after I left. It was a great time. He was very sweet when I first arrived because I had fallen ill the night before and flew to Costa Rica with a fever. He booked us a nice hotel for the night and let me sleep for a solid few hours and took me out for a nice meal to feel better. I'm telling you all of this because I feel horrible that he and I had a falling out after that trip. Typical traveler's miscommunications, maybe spending too much time together, which could make anyone tiff with each other. Granted, I will never forget that experience with your son. We climbed at a spot in Costa Rica that was probably one of my hardest climbs. He always talked me through it. He even left me hanging in the air until I finished because he knew I could do it. And I did. It's very heartbreaking because we hadn't spoken to each other since that trip and I was meaning to apologize and squash any kind of animosity but unfortunately never got the chance. But regardless, I just want to thank you for your wonderful son. He helped me when I was going through a tough time integrating in Switzerland and in Costa Rica, and he had such an adventurous heart. I am truly and sincerely very sorry for your loss as well as your family. I hope this message sees you well and you can remember that your son touched many people's lives all over the world. xx Laura

I felt perhaps telling his mother I was sorry that I was kind of saying it to Adam as well. Adam's mother's response was as follows:

Hi Laura,

Thank you for your account of your time with Adam. Harry and I are coping with the shock as are his brother and sister and wider family. At times like this our brain seems to protect us from the entire picture because we probably cannot handle it all at once. We are all in pain but can see how blessed we are all to have had nearly 37 years with him.

It helps us to hear and read of all his friends' life experiences with Adam. So I thank you so much for spending the time to write all you did.

Adam never held grudges and was very philosophical about people and very forgiving. He would not have even thought about your disagreement again. He had found his mate in Kate and we feel for her also.

He loved everything adventurous and never wasted a minute. We can all be grateful that his life was so full of great times and many people. Yes, I agree. Adam was a great and patient teacher. He taught me to type and I could help him with grammar and proofreading the "back end" of his programmes he wrote for clients' computers.

In time we will heal.

Thank you again for your care. Love, Kelly and Harry

I felt better from hearing from Adam's family but I wanted to hear from Adam and get his blessing for this book.

[January 17th, 2017: I went to see a medium my family goes to. She's amazing at communicating with people who have passed on. I initially was nervous going to meet with her because I wasn't sure if Adam would come through. Plus, I wasn't sure as to what he'd say and if he was still angry with me or not. Without telling her any details about him or our trip, she held onto a picture of us ziplining together but it was flipped over on the back on her lap.

Adam immediately came through, and it was emotional. She asked, "Do you have any questions?" I said, "I just wanted to apologize and hope he isn't angry with how we left things in Costa Rica." She said, "He's laughing." and said, "that's kid stuff." I felt like I could hear his voice. She said, "He never saw the trip as bad or negative and for me not to worry about it. And he doesn't have any ill feelings towards me." She said Adam was quite inventive in how he lived his life. She said he flew by the seat of his pants and lived life to the max. She said, "He just laughed and said you wouldn't be able to handle him or his lifestyle." I laughed and thought, what a dick, but Adam knew what he wanted in life and enjoyed the fuck out of it. She mentioned he apologized for his behavior during the trip and he said, "I was outright rude." She said, he knows and apologizes to you for that. I was relieved and emotional for his apology and forgiveness.

I was still quite upset that I didn't know what happened to him, and she said she couldn't tell me but she knew there was a head injury involved. I somehow imagined he died from a skydiving accident or something because he was always doing crazy shit and thought at least he went out doing what he loved. Since writing this book, I had a hard time writing this chapter because I felt like I didn't have the closure and / or didn't know if he would be upset about me writing about our trip both the good and bad. She closed her eyes, held the picture of us ziplining together, and said, *"He's laughing and flattered. He loves the idea of the being in your book."* I said, *"I'll change his name, if he wants."* She stopped me and said, *"No, he wants you to use his name. He wants people to read about him."* I felt a sense of a relief. I needed to hear from him. And he did an amazing job coming through to her.

[I found out a couple months later from Prof, the guy who came with us climbing in Switzerland, that he was hit by a train. It isn't known if it was deliberate or not, but there wasn't a note left of any kind. His friend told me to think of him in the good times we all had. So, thank you Adam for all you've taught me. You've taught me I can conquer my fears and live a life to the max. You were one crazy motherfucker in the best way, and I am happy I met you. I feel you like you'd laugh and agree with me. So cheers to you, and we'll meet again someday.]

Chapter 10: A Joke Turns Into Love

2015

"The best things in life are unexpected because there were no expectations."-Eli Khamarov

Upset about Mark and I, I went on a few more dates with Carter. I felt like he was perfect for me in some way because he was into spirituality and he was knowledgeable, plus he was a traveler too. I fell for it *again*. I fell in love with his words and not his actions.

After being home for a few days, I was settling in and relaxing after a long trip. Carter called me and we were discussing our families. As the conversation went on, he said, "You come from a broken home because of the addiction issues your brother struggled with and your parents are divorced." I was shocked as to what I just heard. I sat in silence for a few moments to gather my thoughts. When I was away in Costa Rica, he was talking sweet nothings to me. I was angry.

I said, "I don't come from a broken home." Previous to our talk, I had visited his home and noticed his parents were married but slept in separate rooms. I felt judged and violated in a sense because he said what he needed to say in order to sleep with me.

He was the straw that broke the camel's back. I was fed up with getting into situations where I was left disappointed and heartbroken. I vowed to myself to be picky about who I let into my life. I told myself it's okay to be selfish about whom I choose to love because I should be. I needed to value myself more. I told Carter, "I'm no longer interested in speaking with you because you outright disrespected me and my family." He did not want to let it go, to the point where it became a little scary and strange.

He said, "But I have a gift for you."

I said, "I don't want any gifts from you. It's no longer necessary." In the background on the phone, it sounded like he was in the car driving somewhere. I could hear the wind whooshing in the background. I grew anxious thinking he was driving to my house.

He said, "It's a book. I spent over a week making it while you were in Costa Rica."

I said, "Okay, but I don't want it." He insisted. I said, "If you really want me to have it, then you can mail it to me."

The next morning, I was talking to my brother Stephen about the conversation I had with Carter last night, and I said he was very "Ted Bundy-ish." As Stephen was walking outside to smoke a cigarette, he said, "You have a package on the doorstep from Carter." I thought how is that possible? I looked at the envelope and it didn't have any postage on it.

I yelled to Stephen, "This is what I'm talking about. Creepy!"

Stephen said, "I was up late last night smoking a cigarette around 3:00 or 4:00 a.m.." My brother and I were up talking around 9:00 a.m., so we assumed he'd dropped it off at my house at some point in the middle of the night.

I opened the package and it was a scrapbook of our last five dates. I had an unpleasant feeling as I started to sift through the pages. It was every detail right down to the type of beer we drank when we first met, our text messages printed out, pictures I had taken while I was in Costa Rica to the last page where it had all the details of my upcoming birthday party I was having at my house that he found on my facebook page. I was worried he'd come to my house and make a scene.

The day of my birthday party, I let my friends and family members know of the situation in case he decided to show up. My cousin, Sophia, told me she was bringing her friend Erik. I remembered him from a few months back when we all hung out a bar with her friends. I said, "Oh, yeah I remember him. He was cool."

Erik was in the car with Sophia, and I said, "Tell him he may need to be security for the night or play fake boyfriend if this guy shows up." I could hear Erik in the background telling Sophia, "Tell her, it's not my fault if she decides to keep me." I laughed it off and thought, *Yeah, okay, buddy.*

Erik and I didn't get to interact much at my party but he caught my eye more so than last time. Without even knowing him yet, I noticed how he carried himself with confidence and masculinity. He was wearing a gray kangol cap with a beige trench coat. He walked up to my father, introduced himself, and then came up to me and said, "Happy birthday," gave me a kiss on the cheek and handed me a bottle of champagne.

He was smooth but not in an arrogant way. We all sat by the bonfire, drinking, laughing, and having a good time. Stephen and his friend are chefs, and they were in the kitchen making a delicious dinner that looked straight from Iron Chef. I was enjoying my friend's company, but out of the corner of my eye, I could tell Erik wanted to speak to me. I said, "Come walk with me to my slackline." I wanted to show off my skills despite having a few drinks. He held my hand to stabilize me and I was able to walk most of it but fell off. He caught me and I felt he wanted to kiss me right there but a friend of mine walked over and ruined the moment. I laughed it off and suggested we all go back to grab a drink and sit by the fire.

***

Carter never did show up but the potential made me uneasy. Days later, I received novel length text messages, which were a mix of insults and him professing his love for me. I went to the Bronx for a night out with Sophia and her girlfriends to get my mind off of Carter's craziness. Sophia said, "Let's text Erik to see if he can come." I immediately said yes, since I liked our interaction at my birthday party. Erik came and was looking handsome as ever. I was a little buzzed and felt more comfortable flirting with him. I put my hand on his knee and asked, "Want to go play darts?" I told him to play first. He was hitting the board and I walked behind him, put my hands in the front of his chest, and said, *Now try.* He threw the dart right into the bull's eye.

Carter's texts continued throughout the night, Sophia came up with the idea to take pictures of me and Erik as a joke to look like were dating and "in love" to post on my social media to hopefully give him the hint to back off. As we took photos, Erik and I had a surprised look on our faces. I said, "Damn, we actually look kinda good together." Erik looked at me and winked. As the night was coming to an end, Erik drove me back to my car, but I wasn't fit to drive. We dropped off Sophia at my car and she asked, "Are you coming with me?"

I laughed and whispered, "He wants to take me home." Which wasn't true.

Sophia said, "Take care of my cousin and don't be a dick. I'll come get her in the morning."

He laughed and said, "Of course, she's in good hands."

I traveled all over the world and fantasized meeting someone abroad who was *similar* to me. Yet, the person I would end up falling for was not only in the same country as me but practically in my own background, an hour away from me. I convinced myself I should be with someone who's just like me, who's a nomad and wants to hop around figuring out how to make money doing what we love without the nine to five grind sitting in a cubicle. I realized when dating people who were just as spontaneous as me, I didn't feel secure because the relationship didn't feel stable. In relationships, I always used to feel trapped. Trapped where I felt like I had to stop my travel plans because who would want to date a traveler like me? I was scared to believe another person who said they would accept me as a traveler. I held myself back from true love, when deep down that's all I ever wanted.

Erik wasn't like the others I've met during my travels. He is a no bullshit, shoot it to ya straight kinda guy. He definitely didn't sugar coat things, yet he was kind and gentle. We moved slow and took our time to get to know each other, which was something I wasn't used to. Despite moving fast, the first night drunk in lust, I didn't feel the need to question how he felt about me because he continuously *showed* me.

I've learned there's no rules when it comes to love. I was in a place where I was over bringing men into my life who didn't add to it. I chose to stop choosing men who wooed me with their words while their actions couldn't show for it. I chose to fall in love with myself and have no expectations because it leads to disappointments; the less you expect from life and people, the less disappointed you will be. It will bring excitement to your life, it's like getting surprise gifts taking you on a new journey every day. Before meeting Erik, I wanted to give up on love. But a joke turned into love. He always created the space for me to be me and I felt free.

Four years later, being entangled in his arms and his energy is something I can't describe. Comfort, safety, warmth, and filled with love. Lots of kisses, laughs, and I-love-you's. We embarked on our biggest adventure of finding a place to call our own and recently we got engaged. We choose each other every single day. We have each other's back and have the confidence in each other to fulfill our dreams. We are not the same, which I see as a blessing. We challenge each other to grow and step outside of our comfort zones. We can't promise each other forever but we can for today. He teaches me to be present and to see the good in everything. He hasn't traveled as much as me but he wants to see the world *with* me. So we decided to make that happen.

From our first trip together to Montreal, road tripping to Maine, camping in upstate New York, going to Cuba and exploring places in our own backyard. We vowed to each other we'd take as many trips as we could whether it's far or near. This is different for me because I'm not used to staying put and it's challenging to be comfortable with the idea of setting down roots. For the first time, I fell in love with a man's actions versus his words. We hope and plan to continue on this adventure spiritually within together and go abroad to many places around the world.

Chapter 11: Traveling Free Isn't Always Better

2016

Taglit: The Hebrew word for "Discover."

Being Jewish and Catholic, I didn't feel a connection to either religion. I heard about the birthright trip to Israel but honestly didn't feel it was for me because I wasn't close to being Jewish despite having a Jewish last name. I was coming up on my twenty seventh year, which is the cut off to go on this trip. At the last minute, I decided to apply and go for it. My father is Jewish and my mother is Catholic. They are not too religious, and although they tried to pass down their religious views when I was little, according to my mom I was not a fan of either. While researching my Italian ancestry, I came to love the process of figuring out the missing puzzle pieces of who I am and where I came from. As excited as I was to find out where I came from on my mother's side, I felt a missing piece to the puzzle of where I came from on my dad's side.

My father was born in Buenos Aires, Argentina, and I never heard him talking about Jewish culture other than some Yiddish words here and there. I wasn't looking to convert, but I wanted to have an open heart to hear what being Jewish was all about. I wanted to do it all; Shabbat, breaking the bread, being amongst other Jewish people who were on the same journey as me to connect. Birthright gives individuals with a Jewish heritage a chance to go back to the motherland and learn about Jewish culture. Birthright let's Jews fly for free to Israel on a group tour for ten days.

The day before flying out to Israel, Erik and I moved in together. We were scrambling to move and I was trying to prepare for my trip the next day. Stressed was a bit of an understatement. The next morning, Erik drove me to JFK airport, and as we were getting closer, the reality was setting in that we wouldn't see each other to the next ten to eleven days. We arrived a little bit before 7:00 a.m. and had a few moments to say goodbye. We hugged and kissed, and he said, "Please be safe, I love you." I walked inside and saw a big group of people and I assumed it was Birthright. It was, but our group leaders hadn't arrived yet. I always heard Israeli security was intense and wasn't sure what I'd experience, let alone forty of us being questioned. I thought we'd be there forever. Finally, I was called over and he asked random questions. "How many passports do you have? What's your mother's maiden name? Do you have a Hebrew name? Did you get ever go to Hebrew school? When was the last time your dad went to synagogue?

I couldn't answer a majority of these questions, and I couldn't help but laugh. I thought I was failing miserably and he wouldn't let me on the plane. He then asked, "What is your favorite holiday?"

I said, "4th of July."

He laughed and shook his head, "How about a Jewish one?"

I laughed and said, "Hanukkah?"

"Are you even Jewish?" he asked.

I said I was.

He said, "So why are you going to Israel for birthright?"

I laughed and said, "Clearly, I don't know shit about being Jewish."

He said, "Touché," and let me through security.

My ticket said it was standby, and I thought, *That can't be good. I hope I get a seat on this plane.* Luckily, I was able to get a seat but it was a window seat. I love the aisle because it forces me to get up and stretch, plus I'm not squished inside between people the whole flight. I overheard one of the girls complaining she wanted a window seat. I told her I'd gladly switch if her ticket happens to be an aisle. I was praying it was an aisle seat, so when we were boarding, I saw her behind me and I yelled out, "What seat do you have!" She said, "Aisle!" We switched and I got a better seat, sitting in the front row in the exit row. There was plenty of legroom for this twelve-hour flight.

A woman sitting in between me and another woman had such an incredible laugh. We all had our seats back with blankets and looked at each other and we all busted out laughing. The woman laughed and said, "This feels like first class." I already felt a sense of relief to be sitting next to these women for the next twelve hours. I told them about my seat situation and how at the last second I got moved.

She said, "Nothing is a coincidence."

We all exchanged names. The woman with the infectious laugh was from Israel visiting her family and her name was Shira, and the other woman's name was Michelle and she was going there for business.

Shira was such a free spirit. She said, "I feel so free and love to travel and meet people. I'm curious about the world and other people's cultures."

A part of me envied her free spirit because it reminded me of how I used to be. I was in a bad headspace prior to coming to this trip, I was working in the mental health field which drained me, and I was getting paid minimum wage. I hoped this trip would give me the boost I needed to feel like a traveler again.

We were talking about life and I found out she's in the mental health field, too. I said, "but my true passion is traveling and writing. If I could make money from that, I'd quit my job in a heartbeat." I was watching a movie about some guy who was a skier trying to get into the Olympics. She said, "Pay attention because there's a good message in regards to your passions." She said, "The movie's message is when you want something that bad and you feel it in your gut 100%, then you can have it." She continued to say, "I can't do something that doesn't feel right in my soul."

I said, "I believe in that very much. But it's difficult when you have to get a real job to pay the bills."

She said, "You can be serious but still follow your dreams. I am always smiling and love surprising people, and I'm always flying."

I said, "My mom would say that about me and my brother, that we were born with wings."

Shira said, "I LOVE that! And when I have kids, I'm going to raise them to have wings. But my mom doesn't understand my lifestyle with wings." I understood what she meant. She said, "You know, my mom gave me life but she doesn't own me. She can't walk in my shoes."

When we landed in Tel Aviv it was 5:30 a.m. in the morning. I was exhausted from only being able to sleep on the plane for two hours and being up since 7:00 a.m. the previous day. We grabbed our bags and met the founder of Birthright. I was tired, hungry, and anxious. He was talking about something, but I could barely hear him and my mind tuned out. My anxiety was rising and I was trying to focus on calming down. The leaders told us we would have a full day ahead. Already, I did not like how this sounded. I hadn't done group travel since 2007 and I'd been traveling mostly on my own since then, so I was not used to being on a strict schedule. I started to question whether this would be a good trip or not.

The rest of the day was a blur because we all were tired and jetlagged. I was not prepared for the heat in Israel. I was told by friends back home who have traveled to Israel that the heat was comparable to back home. I was not prepared though, for a heatwave in what's already a hot Israel. From what I do remember, we stopped at a gas station to have lunch. I wouldn't eat lunch at a gas station back home. I wanted to experience true Israeli cuisine. We quickly got back on the bus after scarfing down whatever we could find to drive to Caesarea where there were ancient ruins.

The heat was unbearable, and I was over it like many others in the group. They kept pushing us to walk around and tell us history about the place. After, most of us tried to get some sleep but I couldn't get into a comfortable position long enough before the leaders said, "We're going to go on a two-hour hike. So prepare yourselves now before we get there." All I wanted was a bed and a shower. I was still in my clothes I had left New York in. Ira, our tour guide, was quite the talker. The hike was strenuous and felt like it was never going to end.

After our hike, we drove to our hostel in Shlomi. We showered, ate, and got situated in our rooms. The leaders came around and said, "We have another activity." He pulled out a ball of red yarn string. He said, "My name is Ira, and the first letter in my name is "I" and I will say something about myself. I am intelligent." He continued, "You all will do the same but I want you to add where you went to school, what you studied, and then throw the ball of yarn to someone else."

After throwing it around a few times, the string began to create a web of criss-crosses. He said, "Find the person you are connected to from the string. I will come around and cut the string long enough for you to wrap twice around each other's wrists. You are to wear them until they fall off." After everyone had their bracelets, we all anticipated leaving and going to bed. Ira said, "Meet me in the bomb shelter (basement) for a talk about our plans for tomorrow."

Everyone huffed and puffed our way down to the bomb shelter (which were everywhere in Israel). Ira would only tell us the plans for the next day and what time we had to wake up. People were leaning on each other in delirium. Ira was talking but I don't think anyone was processing anything.

Someone asked, "So what time are we waking up?" That would be the theme for every talk we had with Ira. Ira said, "6:15 a.m."

Everyone let out a big sigh.

We woke up early, and semi-rested, we went to eat breakfast. We brought food we could fit in our backpacks and stole toilet paper rolls from our hostel rooms because there were never any bathrooms nearby on the trails. The Hatzbani Nature Reserve is a hike with streams and creeks. The river eventually runs into the Jordan River. The water was cold but it felt refreshing in between my toes. Ira told us more stories about Israel along the way. I enjoyed hearing about Israel from another perspective other than the news back in the states.

We went to Mount Bental that had gorgeous panoramic views of Golan and the border of Syria. From the view, I could see the fence to Syria. It may sound silly, but you expect to see a warzone, which I'm sure in some parts it is, but in this area there was nothing but nature's beauty. We hear about chaos from our media, and we become unconsciously judgmental and fearful of these countries, even Israel, but to see it in person was humbling. Ira pointed out a small UN building in the near distance and mentioned it was under siege from ISIS a week ago. Everyone was in shock. To think ISIS was here not too far from where we stood only a short time ago, was hard to comprehend from what we are conditioned to know and think of ISIS in the states.

Ira stopped us for a moment and said, "I want you guys to all write any problem you may be having that you want to get rid of." I hated my job back home, and I wanted to find a way to make my dreams come true of being a writer. He said, "Put it in this bag and at the end of the trip, I will ask you if you want to keep it or leave it here in Israel." We all wrote problems we wanted to get rid of on small pieces of paper and put it in his bag. He said, "Ok, now that we are rid of our problems, let's move on!"

We then went back to the hostel to prepare for Shabbat. We lit the candles, held each other in a circle, sang songs, and blessed the wine. The Shabbat ceremony was one of my favorite parts of the trip so far. We said a prayer over the Challah bread and each took a piece before we had dinner. Ira said, "Eat quickly because we have more activities in the bomb shelter." Ira set up chairs for us to sit in a big circle, which we always did. Ira dropped the bomb on us that we had to be up at 5:45 a.m. tomorrow. We all looked around at each other confused because it was Shabbat and tomorrow was the day of rest. He laughed at our confusion and said, "Meet up at 10:45 a.m." We all cheered; we could finally sleep in. Being in a group of forty-seven people with 47 different personalities is a lot to deal with. I don't mind being social but I like to have my alone time where I can relax or write about my travels. So, I took full advantage of having an early night and catching up on rest tomorrow because I was sure we wouldn't get another sleep-in day for a while.

***

Rest day was fantastic to say the least. I slept in until the last minute before we had to meet up. Ira took us to the forest to do a group activity with a beachball that had questions taped to it. Some of the questions were: "If you had a yacht, what would you name it? If you were on a deserted island, who and what would you bring?" We bumped into some Israeli soldiers who stopped to watch us play. They sat against their military tanks. A week into this trip, and it was funny how quickly I became accustomed to a heavy military presence and it strangely was calming to know if anything happened, someone would know what to do. A majority of the group went to take pictures with the soldiers and their tanks. I was going to, but then I decided not to.

Sometimes, I don't want to take pictures when I travel, I like to sit back and soak it in. I prefer to write about my experiences in great detail, which is better than any picture I could take. I have the words to describe the day where it immediately brings me back, and I can picture exactly what was going on. Pictures are great, but when you have long travel days you tend to forget the little details and writing fills in the blanks. I wouldn't have been able to write this book based off of pictures but I have two travel journals filled with each day I traveled. I was able to remember details from over twelve years ago that probably would have been lost.

Next, Ira wanted to see how much we identified as being Jewish. There were blue circles which represented being Jewish, the red circles for being American and the green circles for you and how you felt about yourself. The size and distances from each circle on the cards represented how connected you felt to each one. I picked green and red circles of the same size and a small blue circle. I said, "I wanted the green one to be a little bit bigger and the red to be smaller. I wanted the American to be a little smaller because I don't relate with nationalism. And the small blue circle was away from the other two because I don't feel a strong connection to being Jewish but I want to." We listened to everyone's version of how they identify themselves.

Ira said, "I hope as time goes on here that the blue circles you all have will be bigger."

We arrived back at the hostel to change and prepare for the Havdalah ceremony, which means "separation" and it marks the end of Shabbat; it's performed before nightfall. We stood in a circle, lit a candle, and one of the girls from the group went around to check our nails to make sure they weren't dirty to signify we didn't work and had our day of rest. During the Shabbat, Jews believe they receive an extra soul at the beginning of Shabbat and by the end we lose a soul. Another person went through with sweet spices, which consisted of cloves, cinnamon or bay leaves. It is believed to bring the sweetness into the next week. Then they dipped the candle into the wine after someone sipped it. We dipped our pinky finger in the wine to either put behind our ears or in our pockets for good luck and good fortune.

We dragged ourselves out of bed the next morning for a two-hour hike to Mount Meron. It was beautiful, but because it was hot, the importance of staying hydrated in the desert heat with an ongoing heatwave was vital. I was growing tired of the non-stop activities with little rest in between. One of the girls in the group would refuse to come down for some activities, and stay in her room. The leaders would have to convince her join us. I felt her pain.

I understand Birthright wanting to jam pack this trip with things to do but it takes away from the experience. I'd rather see a handful of things and spend a lot of time in each place rather than hopping around. The girl eventually came down and we drove to another destination to a town called Tzfat where they told us we would do a four-five hour walking tour. We stopped a small synagogue where half of us were falling asleep from the warmth and exhaustion of hiking and walking all day.

We left the sweatbox synagogue and walked to a park. The leaders said, "We have some Israeli popsicles so you guys can cool off. But we want you all to sit and close your eyes for a moment and meditate while you eat your popsicle." I thought, *what kind of weird shit is this?* But we did it and they said, "Okay, now open them!" Seven Israeli soldiers appeared in front of us. The leaders said, "They will now join us on the rest of our trip. So please get to know them and ask them any questions you like about Israel." We were on day four of our trip and they'd accompany us for the next six days.

We listened to their stories as each of them introduced themselves and told us which positions they held in the military. They were young, some close to my age (26) or younger. The leaders said, "The soldiers will walk with you to find lunch but hurry because we have very little time to eat. We have to be back on the bus at 1:15 p.m." It was 12:50 p.m., we broke into little groups and we asked the soldiers where we could grab food fast. We found a falafel stand and we ate our sandwiches as we walked back to the bus. We had a three-hour drive to Jerusalem.

When we arrived at our hotel, we went straight to dinner, which was a step up from the dinners we'd been having. This tasted more like authentic Israeli food if I had to guess. We ate quickly and met down in the bomb shelter to have a history lesson on the Israeli and Palestinian conflict. The leaders said, "It won't be long, just an hour." I laughed to myself and thought, *the conflict has been going on for thousands of years, there's no way we're gonna be able to talk about it for an hour.* We also had seven Israeli soldiers with us who I assumed would have strong opinions as well. We discussed what we Americans thought the solution should be. What was interesting was the

Israelis seemed be just as confused as we were as to how to stop the conflict.

Emotions were running high the last few days being in Israel. Learning about the conflict from their perspective and talking with the Israeli soldiers about their daily lives and being in the military. The leaders told us, "We will soon go to Yad Vashem, the Holocaust museum. We want you guys to mentally prepare for it because it can be emotional." I visited the one in Washington D.C., and I thought it was intense but from what I heard this one takes the cake.

Two parts in particular struck me hard and I wasn't expecting to get as emotional as I did. I think being in Israel and learning more about myself, and being Jewish, the museum hit me harder than usual. As I walked into one of the exhibits, there was a video playing of an old man who survived standing in a pit as a young boy with his grandfather where they were about to be shot. Nazis held up their guns and told them to turn around. The Nazis cocked their guns and the grandfather started reciting the "Hear, O Israel" prayer, and the Nazis shot his grandfather.

The grandfather fell on top of the young boy and the Nazis thought the he was dead too, but he made it. The young boy, now an old man, started to tear up telling this story, and I lost it. I couldn't imagine the feeling of knowing this could be your last day on Earth and to witness your loved one being killed with his body on top of yours. The fear he must have felt knowing he was alive and hoping the Nazis wouldn't notice must have been paralyzing. All these years later, it was still raw as if it happened yesterday.

The museum is designed specifically to make you feel certain emotions as you walk through. For example, in the beginning it's a comfortable room with carpet, and as you walk to the main part it turns to cement and the structure is in an A frame shape, and as you look out it looks like the walls are slowly moving inwards. The second part was this dark room filled with mirrors and five candles were lit in the middle of the floor. When you walked in, the reflection of the candles on the mirrors looked as if a million candles were lit, signifying how many children died. Tears rolled down my face as I saw it, and as you walked around the candles in the middle a loudspeaker came on with the voices of children saying kids' names, their age, and where they were from. All of them were killed.

We all left in a somber mood. Ira said, "We've had an emotional day, let's all go sit in the park, play an activity, and relax." I don't think anyone was up for any activities at this point. We all sat in a circle on the grass. We kicked off our shoes and enjoyed a cooler day. Ira said, "Turn to the person next to your and massage their back and then switch sides." We all smiled in relief after a long emotional day.

We headed back to the bus to get ready for our night out, which I wasn't looking forward to because we had to be out until 11:00 p.m. and then had to wake up at 6:00 a.m. Normally, I liked to go out, have a couple drinks, and have a fun time, but being hungover the next day and going on hikes in desert heat wasn't ideal. I went downstairs to look for everyone and couldn't find them. I bumped into one kid from my group and asked, "Where is everyone?"

He said, "They're down the hall waiting by the door." I walked down the hall and no one was to be found. The leaders prided themselves on never leaving anyone behind, but they did with me. And I was honestly relieved.

I went back to my room and broke down. I called my mom back home and needed to hear a familiar voice. I told her, "I want to go home, I miss home, I miss Erik and everyone. I hate how this trip is going. And I still have six days left." I didn't like how much we were doing each day with barely any breaks and running on little sleep. I cried and told her, "I hate traveling like this. There's too many people and I just want my alone time. And I can't get away from anyone." I was tired of being on a strict schedule with too many rules to follow. This is not traveling, at least not to me

My mom tried to console me the best she could over the phone and said, "Try to make the best of it. And see them leaving you behind as a blessing in disguise. Take your alone time and get an early night." To feel like I did something on my own, I asked the hotel concierge if there were any stores open nearby to grab snacks. I felt like a little kid breaking the rules and I felt vindicated.

A majority of the group woke up obliterated and hungover. We drove to Mt. Herzl, which is Israel's national cemetery for the fallen soldiers. I enjoy visiting cemeteries around the world. They are all so unique and some are even beautiful to walk through compared to ones we have in the US. Ira told us stories of the lives of some of the young men and women who fought for their country. I was shocked how young they all were, and some of them were even American. Even a few Americans who came on their Birthright trip, fell in love with Israel and joined the military.

Eitan was our medic and security who accompanied us throughout the whole trip. He came up to speak about his story. Eitan was a young man, skinny in stature with curly brown hair which had a mind of its own. He started telling us how when he was out in the field driving his military tank, his fellow soldier and friend was complaining he wanted to sit by the window. Eitan cleared his throat, his voice was beginning to crack from holding back tears. They switched seats and two seconds later they were hit by a missile. Eitan walked away unscathed with maybe minor scratches, but his friend died. He was struggling to get the words out telling us the rest of the story.

We all could feel his pain and sadness, and a lot of us in the group, the soldiers and myself began to cry for him. Eitan continued and said, "I blame myself. That missile was meant for me." He continued, "My friend's family ignores me when they see me and blame me for the death of their son." He sobbed. One by one all of us went up to him and gave him a hug.

The other graves had pictures and colorful decorations. You can tell their families took great effort to not only visit their loved ones but to make sure it showed who this person was. Ira said, "Ok, off to the next activity." I struggled to get up and leave onto the next activity planned after something so emotional. We went to the market in Jerusalem, which was everything and more from dry teas and spices to fresh fruits and meats. I didn't have much of an appetite and didn't want hot food, so I found a smoothie stand instead, which I hoped would hold me over, especially with all the water I was drinking. We had a water drinking schedule. By noon, we should have already drunk three to four liters of water. Some days I drank seven and still felt dehydrated.

After the market, we drove to the Dead Sea, which is the lowest place on Earth. The leaders warned us on the bus, "Be aware that it may be even hotter here, so drink your water and make sure to put sunblock on." *Great.* I thought. My energy was depleted, and for some strange reason I didn't expect the water to be as warm as it was. It felt like walking into a hot tub. We didn't spend much time there other than floating in the water, which was amazing to feel.

When we got back to the hotel, I was feeling dizzy and overly hot. I sat at dinner and started getting tunnel vision, I left my plate and walked out of the cafeteria to find Eitan to let him know I need to get to my room as soon as possible. Eitan said, "Are you alright?"

I said, "No, I feel really hot but I also have the chills. I feel like I can't cool off and I may pass out."

Eitan opened the door to his room that had two twin beds, "You may have heat exhaustion. Lie down for a minute and I'll run you a cool shower." I went to shower and it didn't help much. A few minutes later, I walked out and he said, "Did that help?"

I said, "Not really, I still feel hot." Eitan said, "Lie down, rest, and drink water. You probably need food, too. I'll let the leaders know." Eitan texted them and laid in the bed adjacent to keep an eye on me and distract me from worrying. Any time you are sick abroad, it's probably one of the worst feelings. I texted my dad and Erik back home to let them know what was going on.

There were a few girls who were hospitalized from dehydration a few days earlier. I didn't want to go to the hospital unless it was absolutely necessary. Eitan said, "Please eat something, you'll be okay. And I'll walk you to your room, we have an early day tomorrow." The next morning, we had to be up at 4:00 a.m. to do our biggest and toughest hike at

Masada.

On top of girls getting hospitalized for dehydration, our group was hit with a nasty stomach bug. Some people were hospitalized because of that, too. I prayed I wouldn't get it. I was nervous being we all were in such close quarters all the time. I felt like we all were slowly dropping like flies. Luckily, I didn't get it, but one of the soldiers got it, and she was surprised since she never had been sick with a stomach bug in Israel before. She was in my room, and the she was yacking her brains out all night. She wound up staying behind and went to the hospital in the morning while we got ready to hike Masada. The hardest trail, called the Snake path, was canceled due to the excessive heat so we lucked out and did the easy trail. We saw hundreds of Israeli soldiers ahead of us and we asked some of them, "What are you guys doing?" They said, "We've been training since 10:00 p.m. last night and Masada is our last stretch. We've been walking and training for about twenty-five miles."

The goal was to get up as early as we did to reach to the top so we can watch the sunrise, but it was difficult with all the soldiers ahead of us. I wasn't sure if would make it, but we did, and it was worth waking up early and hiking up this damn mountain. Hiking down the mountain was a lot easier than going up and we jumped back on the bus to head to the Bedouin tents where we were going to sleep outside in the desert for a couple nights.

When we arrived a couple hours later, Ira said, "I'm afraid, I have some bad news. They overbooked and we don't have a tent for tonight. It's possible we'll have to sleep outside."

Scorpions are a real thing out here, so a lot of us were unhappy. We were told to put our stuff into another tent for now, until they try to figure out a sleeping situation. We went to dinner in another tent where we sat on pillows. Delicious meats, rice, warm pita bread and hummus came out on huge silver platters. It was the best food I had so far. The Bedouin tents were specifically for Birthright groups, there were other groups there on different tours. They had a concert going on and we all did the Horah, it was fun but I couldn't help but wonder when we'd get to sleep since we've been up since 4 am and it was getting close to midnight.

There were designated activities to go to, and I chose meditation. A guy from my group and I were trying to look for it but couldn't find it at all. We both looked at each other laughing at how tired we were and we both said to each other, "Should we just ditch it?" We eventually found it hidden behind another tent. The meditation was so long, we both fell asleep.

We woke up from our meditation nap and walked back to our group. Ira said, "Come, come, form a circle please everyone. So, the tent we put our stuff in is actually our tent." It was a joke they overbooked it. We all gasped, laughed, and sighed in relief we had a tent to sleep in. We had thick foam mattresses that resembled futon cushions. I used my book bag as my pillow and the next morning, we all were pleasantly surprised that we slept well for the first time on this trip. The leaders laughed, "That always happens on these trips. We think it's being outside."

We set out for another hike and we were growing suspicious of Ira. Was he a machine? Or perhaps a camel? (Because he barely drank water). I think he finally caught on that we were all struggling. I still wasn't feeling 100 percent myself and didn't want to be in the sun too long. Ira said, "If anyone is feeling weak or has any doubts for this next hike, then please stay back in the bus." I didn't think twice and said, "Fuck it, I'm not pushing myself anymore to risk getting heat exhaustion again." Myself and a couple others decided to stay back with one of the leaders. We chilled in the AC filled bus and played cards. When the rest of the group came back on the bus, they were dragging their feet. Some of them said, "Good thing you guys didn't come, it was so hot."

***

We drove a short distance to Sderot, which was a hot spot for bombs and missiles a couple years prior. Ira said, "This town only has fifteen seconds after the siren goes off to get into the shelter." We went inside the shelter and were told that if a real threat occurred, they wouldn't be able to leave until it was safe. The shelter was huge, it had games and lots of things to do for kids. We walked into a small room to watch a video, and I felt dizzy again. I got really hot and walked out of the room. Eitan saw me walk out and I said, "I'm not feeling good again and I'm just gonna sit out in the main area to cool off."

To my surprise, three girls came out to the area I was a few moments after me complaining of the same issue. We all laid down on the kiddy foam mats and sprawled out sweating.

We all looked at each other and laughed. I said, "At least, we're all dying together."

***

Homesickness was kicking into high gear at this point in the trip. I was trying my best to enjoy it, but I wasn't, and I felt guilty about it since it was free. I pushed myself to experience everything we were doing and follow the schedule. I was at my breaking point, and I was going to listen to my body for the rest of the days here.

We finally made it back to Tel Aviv, which marked the end of our trip. We went to more markets around the city and we had some free time to walk around on our own. At the second market, I was over it. I tapped out and said, "I'm going to stay here in the bar and enjoy the AC." A girl from the group was feeling dizzy and dehydrated, so I volunteered to stay with her while the leaders went off with the rest of the group. We got kicked out of the bar because they were setting up for a concert. The girl started crying. I said, "What's wrong?"

She said, "I feel so horrible and I don't know what to do. Where can we go now?"

I said, "Don't worry, drink more water and I'll go find another place we can sit." I walked down the cobblestone street to look for another place to sit. I found a pastry shop and I asked the owner, "Do you mind if me and my friend sit in here to cool off. She doesn't feel well."

He smiled and said, "Of course, bring her here."

I walked back to grab her and said, "I found a place, it's right around the corner." The owner pulled up chairs for us and set up a fan for her to sit in front of and he offered us free sweets.

***

We got back to the hotel late and Ira said, "You guys get to sleep in again till 10:00 a.m. and have a beach day for your last day." That's all we wanted. Some good R&R. Being away from the desert was a relief, the ocean was perfect. After a few hours, we went back to our rooms to freshen up to do the bar/bat-mitzvah ceremonies. We had the option of doing a bat-mitzvah in Israel. I initially signed up, but I thought we were going to do it on top of Masada where I saw other groups do it. But we wound up doing in the hotel and so I decided to drop out of it.

Afterwards, we got ready to out for our last night in Tel Aviv. We walked to some bar where they said it would be a half hour walk, but it turned out to be an hour. It was Shabbat, so we couldn't use a car to drive to the bar. We were all sweaty by the time we got there. We got there at 10:30 p.m. and had to leave by 12:20 a.m., and I was annoyed we couldn't even enjoy going out because even going out and having fun was rushed.

It was a cute bar, outdoors hidden in the bushes like a speakeasy. I had one drink and didn't feel like staying. The bar was in a small complex full of other restaurants and bars, so I went to explore until we had to leave. A couple other girls and Eitan joined me where we sat, talked and joked around until the group was ready to leave. We had to walk an hour back but a lot of the group was wasted, and it felt like it took even longer to walk back. My foot was bleeding by the time we got back. We got back to the hotel at 1:30 a.m. and had to be up at 7:00 a.m. for another full day. I give a lot of credit for the kids who did the hikes and walking tours either drunk or hungover. I don't know how they did it.

***

We went to a morning graffiti tour in Tel Aviv, and it was interesting to learn about the many hidden messages behind the art. The guide was American and I assume he must have been from the East Coast, which was great because he hit all the high points of the tour and went through it fast because he saw some of us were struggling after a night out.

When the tour was over, we went to the Jewish Culture Center to have our last discussion together. We did a big circle and all moved in towards the center for a big hug. Then we sat down and had to say three things about the person to our left. One thing about their character, a physical trait you like, and one you take away from them. One of the leaders was sitting next to me, I said, "I love your accent (She was from Chicago), and I take away that you've always kept a positive attitude even when we were all dragging and complaining."

We all discussed how we felt about the trip and what impacted us. Ira gave his last speech and said, "Now you all don't have to worry about getting up early anymore." We laughed and cheered. We said our goodbyes to some people in the group who decided to extend their trip and then we left for the airport.

This trip was emotional, I loved some parts and hated others, it gave me a new perspective on Israel and being

Jewish. I discovered a lot about myself, especially that I don't like hot places, but spiritually I found I am a strong person and I did things that made me uncomfortable. I pushed myself to try everything this trip had to offer but I also had the strength to say no when my body told me enough was enough. I felt a connection with being Jewish I've never felt before. I would love to experience Israel again on my own terms, slow and steady, soaking in the culture and perhaps in the winter time.

Chapter 12: Final Thoughts

2019

"Travel isn't always pretty. It isn't always comfortable. Sometimes it hurts, it even breaks your heart. But that's okay. The journey changes you; it should change you. It leaves marks on your memory, on your consciousness, on your heart, and on your body. You take something with you. Hopefully, you leave something good behind." – Anthony Bourdain

Travel is one of those things that will change your life forever. I started out in a rocky place struggling with anxiety attacks and wanting to see the world. I knew how traveling made me feel when I went to Europe in 2007, and I wanted to *feel* that again. I still struggle with anxiety from time to time but I've come to a place where I fell in love with it, it forces me to reevaluate where I am and reminds me it's time to take care of myself. Does it suck at times, yes, but other times, maybe anxiety is the wrong word but I use the adrenaline to push me forward to get outside of my comfort zone. I learned a lot about myself and the choices I was making in life and love.

Sometimes you have to make bad choices (ok, maybe a lot) in order to recognize what's good out there. The best decision I've made was falling in love with myself. I took a different kind of spiritual journey where I listened to what my body told me, I gained confidence from traveling the world to speak up without a shaky voice.

I became selfish about who I brought and kept in my life and embraced the fact not everyone is meant to be in your life forever. I appreciate every single person I met during my travels whether it was a friend, enemy, or lover. You all taught me something about myself and the world.

Traveling has opened my world to endless possibilities and opportunities to grow as a person. As a reader, I want you to gain the confidence to travel or whatever your heart desires. Live life to the max, even when you're scared shitless, because on the other side of fear lies freedom. Never let anyone tell you you can't do something. Whether you succeed or fail, the vital thing is to try. Because you know what? Life is way too short to be miserable in any aspect of your life.

As for me, I'm currently putting down roots in New York with Erik and building our homebase while I work on making this book, my dream, come true, so I can eventually write and travel the world and show Erik what traveling has to offer. I do not know what the future holds, but we do know what is happening right now in the present moment. The present is the surest thing we have. So, grab on to it. One other thing I know for sure: I will not stop traveling; it's ingrained in my soul. As my mom would say, "You're a child born with wings.

Author Acknowledgements

I want to thank my parents who raised me to be a child with wings. To be independent and always follow my dreams and passions. You've instilled in me that life is too short to be unhappy. You've taught me to work hard and never give up. Thank you for always supporting me through the countless tears and fears that I wouldn't be able to write a book. I did it. I also want to thank my brother and sister for pushing me to travel the world and also to write this book. You have both given me lessons in life and showed me anything is possible. To my Aunt Franny who always gave me that extra push to get going on my book when I was down about if I'd finish or get it published. Thanks for telling me inspiring stories about other authors who struggled in the beginning and who are now wildly successful. And that I, too, can be successful.

To my talented photographer, Jesus Baez who took beautiful photos for my cover and headshots. Your talent and passion astounds me. To my editors, Ransom Patterson, Susan

Gaigher and Keidi Keating, thank you for all your hard work and.making this possible. To Curtis Miller from CM Designs, a kind stranger who I found on Twitter to do the cover design for this book, I'm eternally grateful for your kindness and talent.

To my beta readers, who took time out of their day to read my book and give me constructive feedback. Laura Weller, thank you for your time and dedication to print out my book and mark it up with your feedback. I truly appreciate it. Teddy Herzog, thank you for reading my book and giving me the best of advice of, "Don't tell me, show me." I truly appreciate your opinion and answering questions about life and writing. I can't wait to read your book one day. I value you both deeply.

To all my friends from Kyle Cease's event (you know who you are) and Kyle Cease who met me when I was at my lowest and believed I could become writer. Who still to this day, pushes me to keep writing and believe this dream is possible. I love you all so much.

To all my friends and the people I've met during my travels, you have all shed a light on the pieces of myself to help me grow into a better person. To my therapist, Patricia Hardwick, MSW, LCSW who has become a spiritual motherly figure in my life. You have guided me through the toughest of times in my life when I couldn't see the light. No matter where I am in the world, you go above and beyond to meet with me. You've believed in me and my talents since day one. I'm deeply grateful for your guidance. To my best friend and soulmate, Anthony Rivera, who always inspires me and pushes me to be the best version of myself and is always beacon of light when I need it most.

To my love, Erik who has been my rock since I came home from my travels. You've been such a calming force in my life and you have always embraced the traveler side of me. You've challenged me and pushed me to never give up on my dreams. You've been my biggest supporter and always believed in me. You've taught me to not give a fuck about what anyone else thinks in order to finish this book. I am grateful and happy you are here by my side to see me grow and watch my book become what it is. To many more adventures. I can't wait to be your wife. I love you very much.

About Author

Laura Vaisman was born and raised in New Jersey. In 2007, she was nominated by a teacher in high school to join an educational program to Europe for twenty days and it completely changed her world. More than a decade later, she travels as much as she can with her fiancé, Erik. She continues to write and is now a business owner of her website, Traveling Jersey Girl and Spiritual Nomad where she created a t-shirt line for travelers to be apart of a global tribe and to make sure they don't feel alone, no matter where they are in the world. She will always be a Jersey girl at heart but now resides in Congers, New York with her fiancé.

Made in the USA
Middletown, DE
04 July 2019